W9-CBD-019

THE TASTE
of the
SEASON

DIANE ROSSEN WORTHINGTON

photographs by Noel Barnhurst

THE TASTE
of the
SEASON

INSPIRED RECIPES FOR FALL AND WINTER

CHRONICLE BOOKS
SAN FRANCISCO

TO MICHAEL AND LAURA

Library of Congress Cataloging-in-Publication Data available.

ISBN 0-8118-3792-0

Manufactured in China

Designed and typeset by Annabelle Gould
Food and set styling by Sandra Cook
Styling Assistants: Melinda Barsales and Elisabet der Nederlanden
The photographer wishes to thank Noriko Akiyama and Sara Johnson Loehmann

Distributed in Canada by Raincoast Books
9050 Shaughnessy Street
Vancouver, British Columbia V6P 6E5

10 9 8 7 6 5 4 3 2 1

Chronicle Books LLC
85 Second Street
San Francisco, California 94105

www.chroniclebooks.com

ACKNOWLEDGMENTS

Ethan Ellenberg, my agent, who is always there with a creative thought

Bill LeBlond, my supportive editor

Amy Treadwell, for her helpful editorial input

Denny Luria, for her friendship, creative thinking, and her sense of humor

Lucy Rimalower, for her research skills and help on a moment's notice

Laurie Burrows Grad, Andy and Kathy Blue, Janice Wald Henderson, Jan Weimer, and Ciji Ware, my cooking colleagues and dear friends, for all of their input

Connie Bryson; Judy Miller; Midori Firestone; Lisa and Steve Hillman; Mary Beth Rose; and Cathi, George, and Harry Rimalower; for being great tasters and critics

And finally, my husband, Michael, and my daughter, Laura, my biggest critics and my biggest fans

CONTENTS

INTRODUCTION

As the late-summer days begin to cool down, my thoughts turn to cooking in my kitchen made cozy by a crackling fire. I'm content to stay indoors and think about creating recipes using the produce and flavors unique to the fall and winter months. Ever since completing *The Taste of Summer,* I've wanted to write a companion book that pays tribute to the cooler seasons. *The Taste of Summer* celebrates outdoor living with its menus for a backyard buffet brunch, a casual beach picnic, and a poolside barbecue, among others. Certainly the seasons that invite me back inside my kitchen merit their own volume as well. This book dedicated to the foods, holidays, and events of the fall and winter is the natural counterpart to my earlier work.

The transition from summer to fall brings many changes. For those who cook for a family, autumn ushers in the routine of a busy back-to-school lifestyle. For everyone who enjoys cooking, fall also means that the barbecue is covered and it's back to indoor cooking. The changing leaves bring with them a welcome variety of seasonal foods in the market. Golden pears and ripe red apples replace melons and juicy peaches and apricots. Fall's harvest naturally unfolds with a colorful array of winter squashes, from butternut to delicata to Hubbard. Bags of fresh cranberries appear, and large white and orange pumpkins and smaller decorative ones soon overflow the produce stands. For me, the appearance of pomegranates and persimmons signals the beginning of the holiday season.

The autumn and winter harvests inspire me to use the seasonal produce and foods available at this time of year. Thinking about what to cook as I shop is both a challenge and a pleasure. Freshly dried fall figs caught my eye one day, resulting in Belgian Endive Salad with Apples, Toasted Walnuts, and Fig Vinaigrette (page 34). Holiday nuts motivated me to think about pesto in a new way, giving rise to Chicken Paillards with Pistachio Pesto Vinaigrette (page 63). When tins of maple syrup appeared next to the nut bins at the produce stand, I came up with my Maple Walnut Tart (page 146).

The foods of autumn also inspire me to create new versions of old recipes. It's fun to tweak a familiar recipe and come up with an entirely new dish. Creamy Breakfast Polenta with Mascarpone and Maple Syrup (page 21) replaces oatmeal as a hearty morning dish. French Onion and Fennel Soup (page 44) updates traditional French onion soup. And Short Ribs with Dried Mushrooms and Fire-Roasted Tomatoes (page 74) incorporates new flavors in a traditional dish.

The crisp weather also motivates me to create heartier dishes, entrées that comfort and satisfy, and I've included many such recipes, best classified as comfort food. These dishes are crowd pleasers, new favorites of my husband and friends, including Crispy Roast Duck with Lavender Honey Sauce (page 69) and Braised Lamb Shanks with Toasted Almond Gremolata (page 79). If you're having a large group of friends over, Polenta Lasagna Bolognese (page 113) is an excellent choice. Serve it with a salad, and you have a complete meal that is satisfying and original.

This book opens with a peek into my "seasonal cupboard." This section provides a range of information about the produce and ingredients that I like to have on hand during the cooler months. Organizing meals is something I truly enjoy doing, so I've also included a selection of menus at the back of the book, suggestions of what to serve for holiday meals and other special events. Use these menus as a jumping-off point for planning your own family events and holiday get-togethers.

For me, autumn and winter are the best time of year. I love the school traditions and holidays, the times when I'm surrounded by family and friends. Whether it's a tailgate party, a school potluck, a Halloween trick-or-treat supper, or Thanksgiving dinner, I take pleasure in the menu planning, the shopping, the food preparation, and the setting of a beautiful table. I know not everyone enjoys all of these steps. But the truth of the matter is that a good holiday party only requires two main ingredients—good friends and good food. If you invite the friends, I can promise you that my recipes will ensure good food. Enjoy.

THE SEASONAL CUPBOARD

The contents of my cold-weather cupboard look very similar to those of my warm-weather pantry, with an array of notable additions. Have the following items on hand for cooking these recipes.

Anchovy paste
Sold in a tube, anchovy paste is a combination of pounded anchovies, vinegar, spices, and water.

Apples
Apples are an important component of cold-weather cooking. Here are a few of the many varieties available:
- *Fuji* apples have reddish highlights on yellow-green skin. Firm, crisp, sweet, and slightly spicy, they are ideal for salads, baking, and applesauce.
- *Gala* apples, with their vibrant red and yellow coloring, are excellent for both cooking and baking.
- *Golden Delicious* have a rich, mellow flavor with firm flesh that holds up when cooking. I use these in pies.
- *Pink Lady* apples have a distinctive tangy flavor. Extremely crisp and dense, they are wonderful for eating fresh and also good for pie baking.
- *Pippins* are tart and firm and hold up well when baked, notably in pies. They have a light green or yellow skin and cream-colored flesh.

Arborio rice
The key to making creamy risotto, Arborio is a variety of short-grain rice from Italy. Constant stirring while cooking helps to release the starch in the grains and create a creamy consistency.

Balsamic vinegar
Imported from Italy, true balsamic vinegar comes from only one region, around the town of Modena in Emilia-Romagna. It can take up to 120 years to age. It has a dark brownish red color and is slightly thicker than other vinegars. For cooking, a commercial vinegar (versus the expensive artisan-produced vinegars) from Modena or nearby Reggio is fine. Check the label for either "API MO" (referring to Modena) or "API RE" (referring to Reggio) to be sure you aren't buying an imitation from another area. Look for a refined sweet-tart balance. If you find the vinegar is too strong and tart, you can reduce it by half or so over high heat to tame the acid and give it a syrupy glaze consistency with a richer, more subtle flavor (see Balsamic Syrup, page 166). Another way to balance it is to add a pinch of brown sugar to each tablespoon. *See also* white balsamic vinegar.

Capers
Whether you choose the small French nonpareil variety or the larger Italian capers, rinse them well to remove excess brine or salt. Capers add a piquant flavor and are great in salads, dressing, or sauces, and as a simple garnish.

Chestnuts
Chestnuts are shiny and turban shaped, with one flat side. Their brown skin is bitter and hard, but once peeled, they make a delicious side dish. Use chestnuts in stuffings, soups, stews, or sauces. Bottled cooked and peeled chestnuts are available year-round, and fresh chestnuts are available in October, just in time for Thanksgiving.

There are two basic rules for cooking chestnuts, whether you're boiling or roasting them. Before cooking, make a crisscross cut in the flat side with a sharp knife. After cooking, remove the shell and inside skin while the chestnuts are still warm, using a sharp paring knife. To keep the chestnuts from cooling as you work, let them sit in warm water; it's difficult to remove the shells once the chestnuts are cool.

Chili paste
Used in Chinese cooking, chili pastes vary widely in terms of heat, flavor, and consistency. Most are made from fresh and dried chiles, vinegar, garlic, and other seasonings, and a little goes a long way. They are available in Asian markets and larger supermarkets.

Chipotle chiles
Actually smoked and dried jalapeños, chipotles are widely available canned in a sauce of garlic, tomatoes, and vinegar, labeled "chipotles en adobo." The chiles are moderately hot and have a distinctive smoky flavor.

Chocolate

- *Bittersweet chocolate* and *semisweet chocolate* are unsweetened chocolate with the addition of varying percentages of sugar and cocoa butter. I use imported Valrhona or Callebaut or domestic Scharffen Berger or Ghirardelli.
- *Milk chocolate* is sweetened chocolate to which milk solids have been added.
- *Unsweetened chocolate* is chocolate liquor, pure chocolate, with no added sugar. It is used in baking to flavor items that have other sources of sweetness. I use Baker's or Hershey's.

Cilantro

Also known as fresh coriander or Chinese parsley, cilantro is one of the most common herbs used in Asian cooking and throughout the world. It has wide, flat leaves and a distinct flavor and aroma that liven up salads, salsas, and fish. Choose bright bunches of cilantro with fresh, crisp leaves and stems.

Couscous

A staple of North African cuisine, couscous is often considered a grain, but it is actually a type of pasta made from finely milled semolina wheat. Look for the quick-cooking variety, which takes only five minutes to prepare. It is available in Middle Eastern markets and health food stores, often in the bulk foods section, as well as in many supermarkets.

Cranberries

Bright red and very tart, cranberries are a favorite complement to heavier meats and poultry because the berry's acidity is a good contrast to rich flavors. With a little creativity, cranberries can add a unique taste to all kinds of dishes from pies, quick breads, and cookies to chutneys, conserves, or even ices. (You can even freeze cranberry juice in ice cube trays and add to glasses of sparkling water or punch.)

Choose fresh cranberries that are firm and plump with a glossy luster. Discard any that are blemished or discolored. Buy a few extra bags to freeze, since cranberries are only in season for a few months but will keep for up to a year in the freezer. Don't defrost them before you cook with them. They will better retain their firmness if they're cooked from frozen.

Cream of coconut

A sweetened coconut milk, cream of coconut is good for desserts and mixed drinks. It is usually found in the drinks section of the market. Coco Lopez is a brand found in many supermarkets.

Cumin

Used predominantly in Mexican and Indian cooking, this spice has a distinct aroma. Cumin is available ground or as light brown seeds that can be toasted and ground. It should be used sparingly, to enhance the flavors of meats and vegetables, not overwhelm them.

Demi-glace

A thick, syrupy liquid made by simmering veal bones, vegetables, and seasonings in water for hours, intensely flavored demi-glace is full of natural gelatin and is often used in brown sauces to accompany meats. You can make your own demi-glace or purchase it at gourmet shops. More Than Gourmet ships containers of its Demi-Glace Gold nationwide (1-800-860-9392).

Dried fruit

Dried cherries, cranberries, figs, apricots, and prunes are good additions to rice pudding, savory sauces, pies, salad dressings, rice, couscous, or stuffings. I like to plump them in boiling water or wine first to bring out their full flavor.

Fennel

Sometimes called anise or finocchio, its Italian name, fennel is similar in appearance to celery but with a large bulb on the end and a faint licorice flavor. The stalks should be fresh, crisp, and solid. The feathery leaves (fronds) are excellent for flavoring soups and salads and as a garnish. Cut the stalks off directly above the bulb and use only the bulb in cooking. Make sure to cut out the tough core.

Feta

Traditionally from Greece, feta cheese is made from goat's or sheep's milk, or a mixture. It is firm, tangy, and salty, although the degree of saltiness depends upon the type purchased. Feta is good in salads and dips and as a garnish for pasta or vegetables.

Fontina

Genuine Fontina cheese comes from the Valle d'Aosta in the northwestern corner of Italy. It is straw colored with a mild delicate flavor, and it melts easily.

Ginger

Ginger, or gingerroot, is a knobby-looking tuber with smooth, golden skin. Used widely in Chinese and Japanese cooking, fresh ginger has become a common ingredient in American cooking as well. Ginger should be peeled; then it can be shredded, grated, or julienned. Do not substitute dried ginger for fresh.

Goat cheese

Once only available imported from France, goat cheese (or chèvre) is now produced by small cottage industries across the country. Most American versions are slightly milder than the European goat cheese that is sold fresh, and they have a soft texture, similar to cream cheese. Fresh goat cheese is good served warm on salads or used as in cold salads and pasta sauces. As goat cheese ages, it becomes stronger and its character becomes more pronounced.

Hoisin

A deep reddish-brown thick sweet and spicy sauce used in Chinese cooking, hoisin sauce is made from soybeans, vinegar, garlic, sugar, chile peppers, and spices. Hoisin is available in jars in Asian markets and most supermarkets. It must be refrigerated once opened.

Honey

The oldest sweetening substance, honey was used long before sugar. There are many types of honey, and they vary in flavor and appearance, ranging from a thin liquid to almost hard, and may be white, golden, amber, varnish-brown, or even black. The most popular types are clover honey and orange honey, both of which are suitable for cooking and baking, but you can find more exotic varieties such as lavender, sage, white truffle, and wildflower at specialty food stores and farmers' markets. Honey helps retain moisture in baked goods, and it can often be substituted for sugar in cooking. Honey should be stored in a tightly sealed container; even so, eventually it will crystallize and harden with age. To soften the honey, place the jar in a bowl of hot water.

Jack cheese

Also called Monterey Jack, Jack cheese, made in California, is a mild, semisoft cheese with a high moisture content.

Jalapeño chile

This bright green inch-and-a-half-long pepper ranges from hot to very hot and is one of the most widely used in the United States. Jalapeños are available fresh or canned and are sometimes seen in their bright red fully ripe state. When working with chiles, always wear rubber gloves, and wash the cutting surface and knife immediately afterward.

Kalamata olives

These almond-shaped Greek olives are rich, salty, and slightly fruity. They are soaked in a wine vinegar marinade, then packed into jars, either pitted or with the pits intact.

Lemons

One of the most versatile citrus fruits, lemons have many culinary uses. A few drops of fresh lemon juice can enhance poultry, fish, vegetables, and baked dishes, and the acid can prevent cut fruits or vegetables from turning brown when exposed to air. The colored part of the peel, which is called zest, is often grated and used for extra flavor. Use only fresh lemon juice.

Limes

Closely related to the lemon, limes are often used as lemon substitutes or for their own unique flavor. The small, thin-skinned green fruit is used throughout the world, especially in juices, cocktails, preserves, salsas, and salads.

Maple syrup

Pure amber-colored maple syrup is harvested when the nights are still freezing but the days are mild. It takes about forty gallons of sap to make one gallon of pure maple syrup. The highest-quality syrup comes from the sweetest, freshest sap. You'll find that the lighter the color, the more delicate the flavor. Traditionally maple syrup is used on pancakes and waffles and in muffins or coffee cake. I like to use it as a sweetener in other dishes as well. Try it in salad dressings, baked beans, or nut tarts, or on plain yogurt or hot cereal.

Mascarpone

An Italian cow's milk cheese that must be eaten very fresh, mascarpone is a delicious creamy dessert cheese, a bit like whipped butter or stiffly whipped cream. It is often sweetened slightly and served with fresh fruit and desserts. It was originally made only in Lombardy and only in the autumn and winter, but it is now available all year-round. There are domestic versions as well, but I prefer the imported Italian product. It is usually sold in small tubs.

Matzo meal

The unleavened bread called matzo is ground to make matzo meal. Traditionally used during the Jewish Passover holidays, when flour is forbidden, matzo meal is available in Jewish markets and large supermarkets year-round. Great for stuffing, bread crumbs, and, of course, matzo balls.

Mozzarella

Regular supermarket mozzarella comes in low-fat and nonfat versions. It has a semisoft, elastic texture and is drier and not as delicately flavored as its fresh counterpart. This type of mozzarella is best used for cooking, and it is popular for pizza and pasta dishes because of its excellent melting qualities. Fresh mozzarella is softer and has a mild, delicate flavor. It is excellent served in salads or on pizza.

Mushrooms

- *Cremino:* This is a type of button mushroom (plural *cremini*) that is brown and has a richer flavor than the white button mushroom. When allowed to grow to its full size, it becomes a portobello.
- *Dried mushrooms:* I like to use dried shiitake, porcini, or morels. Make sure they are tightly packaged. Soak all dried mushrooms in warm water before using, and cut off the hard, knobby stem ends. The soaking liquid can be strained and used to flavor soups and sauces.
- *Porcini mushroom:* Also called cèpes, porcini are pale brown and smooth and have a woodsy flavor. In the United States, porcini are most commonly found dried, imported from France or Italy, but the fresh can be found in the fall in specialty markets, at a price.
- *Portobello mushroom:* Large, dark brown mushrooms, portobellos are the mature form of cremini, a variation of the white mushroom. Portobellos have flat, open caps that can be as large as six inches in diameter, and a dense, meaty texture. The woody stems and the dark gills should be removed. They are good marinated and grilled or roasted.
- *Shiitake mushroom:* The dark brown shiitake mushroom, common in Japanese and Chinese cuisines, is available fresh or dried almost year-round. Shiitakes have tan undersides, a rich, meaty texture, and an intense wild mushroom flavor. Soak the dried mushrooms in warm water before using and cut off the hard, knobby stem ends. The soaking liquid can be strained and used to flavor soups and sauces.

Mustard

Exotic mustards now fill the shelves of American markets, but those most commonly used in cooking are Dijon-style and whole-grain mustards. Dijon mustard is made by mixing ground mustard seeds, white wine, the sour juice of freshly squeezed green grapes, vinegar, and spices. Whole-grain mustards, which are of a more ancient origin, are coarser in texture. The hull of the mustard seed is retained, and it contains a strong enzyme that makes the flavor more piquant.

Olive oil

There are many types of olive oil, each possessing different characteristics determined by the olive variety, the climate and the soil, and the amount of processing involved. Extra-virgin olive oils are cold-pressed, rich, and full flavored. Pure olive oils, from olives that have been heated and pressed to extract the last bit of oil, are milder in flavor. Cold-pressed extra-virgin olive oil is usually fruity, green, and redolent of olives. The cold-pressed oils are wonderful used as a flavoring agent in salad dressings or drizzled over vegetables or bread. However, it's better to use a lighter-style olive oil for cooking and sautéing, so as not to overwhelm the delicate flavors of a dish.

Onions and their cousins

There are two basic categories of onions: dry onions, which are fully mature, with a juicy flesh covered with dry, papery skin, and green onions, which have not fully matured. The "cousins," from garlic to leeks, each has a distinctive onion flavor and its own identity.

- *Chives:* Chives are a dark green, delicate herb with a mild flavor that's terrific in salads. For maximum flavor, finely slice them and sprinkle them over potatoes or light pasta dishes just before serving. They are an excellent garnish on any dish that has onions in it.
- *Garlic:* Garlic is more pungent than onions, especially when raw or too heavily used. It differs from the basic onion in that its bulb is composed of about twelve to twenty cloves nestled inside a papery covering. Garlic is a delicious seasoning enhancer, and its intense flavor and fragrance mellows when cooked or roasted into a paste. Garlic should be creamy white, or with a purplish-red cast, plump and firm. Store garlic in a cool, dry place with adequate ventilation, not in the refrigerator. You can purchase peeled fresh garlic in the refrigerated section of most produce departments. Make sure to keep it sealed airtight in the refrigerator.
- *Leeks:* Leeks are my favorite member of the onion family, for both their natural sweetness and their ability to stand alone as an elegant side dish. They look like large thick scallions and are milder in flavor than garlic and onions. They are ideal in soups, most famously vichyssoise, the classic potato leek soup. I often substitute them when onions are called for because I like their flavor.

  Choose leeks that are free of cuts or wilting and no more than two inches in diameter. Because leeks grow in trenches, they are prone to some grit, which you'll need to remove. First, slice the leek lengthwise and widthwise, stopping before the root end so that the leek will stay together. Run your fingers through the layers as you hold the leek under cold running water. Shake off the water, then chop or slice the leek according to your recipe.
- *Onions:* Yellow and white onions are the most common cooking

onions and are relatively mild. They are used in stews, sauces, meats, soups, and myriad other dishes. Red onions, like scallions, are best served uncooked. They are delicious when marinated with cucumbers in wine vinegar.

- *Scallions, or green onions:* Scallions are immature green onions that have not had the chance to fully develop their bulb. Common in salads, Asian dishes, and as a garnish for soups, they are best raw or lightly stir-fried. For a quick garnish, try clipping scallions with scissors.
- *Shallots:* Shallots have an intense concentrated flavor. I like to use them in sauces as well as glazed whole. Make sure they are not dried out and have no sprouts. They must be peeled before using.

Oranges

Choose Valencia oranges for juicing, navel oranges for peeling and eating. The grated or minced zest will add extra flavor to any dish that has oranges in it. Oranges are great for last-minute desserts, orange juice for dressings, sauces, and marinades.

Pancetta

Pancetta is the same cut as bacon, but it is salted, lightly spiced, and then cured rather than smoked. It can be ordered cubed or sliced thick or thin at some supermarkets and at specialty markets. Regular bacon may be substituted if necessary.

Panko

These Japanese bread crumbs, larger and coarser than Western-style bread crumbs, are actually dried, toasted flakes of bread. They are available in plastic bags in Asian markets and some supermarkets.

Parmesan cheese

Authentic Italian Parmigiano-Reggiano comes from an area of Emilia-Romagna where it is strictly licensed and has been produced in much the same way for almost seven hundred years. The cheese should be straw-yellow in color and have a crumbly, moist texture. Look for the words "Parmigiano-Reggiano" stamped on the rind of the cheese to guarantee the real thing. Store the cheese wrapped in plastic in the refrigerator for up to 3 weeks. It's best to grate Parmesan as needed for the fullest flavor.

Pears

Pears are at their peak harvest throughout the winter. Unlike some fruits, they actually ripen best off the tree, so they are picked when still hard and green. If left to ripen on the tree, their flesh will turn mushy or gritty. Since pears ripen from the inside out, test to see if the flesh near the stem gives easily: if it does, the pear is ready to eat. Try these varieties:

- *Anjou* pears have green skin with a yellowish tint even when they're ripe. They are juicy and hold up well when cooked or baked, and they are also good sliced for salads.
- *Asian or Japanese* pears look more like apples with their rounder shape, but they are remarkably crisp and juicy, with a sweet floral fragrance. They are excellent for eating fresh as well as for cheese plates and salads. They take longer to cook than most other pears.
- *Bartlett* pears are unique in that they change color when they ripen, turning from dark green to light greenish yellow. They are the all-purpose pear, ideal for cooking and eating fresh.
- *Bosc* pears have a distinctive brown skin and long, thin neck. With a sweet cream-colored flesh, they are terrific for poaching, baking, and eating fresh. Firmer than other pears when ripe, Bosc pears need only to be slightly soft at the stem.
- *Comice* is the favorite pear for eating fresh. It is juicy, buttery, and slightly spicy, with a round shape and a yellow-green skin that turns reddish as it ripens.
- *Seckel* pears are very small and ideal for preserves or as decoration in centerpieces and floral arrangements. They have dark green skin with reddish tones and firm flesh.

Pecorino Romano

An Italian hard cheese made with sheep's milk, Pecorino Romano has a very distinctive sharp flavor. Pecorino Romano ranges in color from white to pale yellow and has a sharp, pungent flavor. Use the aged cheese for grating for a stronger flavor than Parmesan.

Pecorino Tuscano

A sheep's milk cheese that is considerably milder than Pecorino Romano, Pecorino Toscano is made throughout Tuscany. Although aged Pecorino Toscano can be grated, it is also good cut into thin crumbly slices over foods. It is similar to Parmigiano, but it's a little creamier and has a distinctive bitter walnut overtone that balances its sweetness, giving it added complexity. Try it with sliced pears and a drizzle of chestnut honey or Balsamic Syrup (page 166).

Pepitas

Used in Mexican cooking, pepitas are raw green pumpkin seeds. They are also sold roasted and salted in bags in Latin markets and large supermarkets. If you can't find the roasted variety, you can toast the raw pumpkin seeds yourself. Simply place the pepitas in a medium skillet over medium heat and toss them for 2 to 3 minutes, or until slightly crisp. Salt them to taste. I like to add these to salads.

Persimmons

First brought to California in the 1800s from Japan, persimmons have a deliciously pleasant taste that has been likened to a very ripe apricot. *Fuyus* look something like a squat tomato and can be eaten like a crisp-hard apple off the tree. No need to cook these: they are great in salads and as a fruit topping. *Hachiyas* are elongated, with a pointed tip, and should not be eaten until they're very soft. They are very astringent when unripe, but they sweeten as they ripen, and the pulp is excellent in puddings and bread.

Persimmons don't keep long after they've ripened. If you're waiting for several persimmons to ripen at once for a pudding or pie, you'll find that each persimmon has its own slightly unpredictable and unique ripening schedule. You can avoid the problem by harvesting the flesh of each persimmon as it ripens; then store the flesh in the freezer in an airtight container until you have the required amount.

Pine nuts

The pine nuts grown in the United States are smaller than their European, Asian, or South American counterparts. Also called *piñons*, pine nuts have a creamy color and a rich nutty taste when toasted. Be sure to use pine nuts fresh, as they go stale faster than other nuts, and store them tightly sealed in a cool place or the freezer.

Pistachios

California has become the second-largest producer of pistachio nuts in the world. The natural color of the shell is grayish white; red pistachios have been dyed for cosmetic reasons. Inside, pistachios have a vivid green color. Shelled unsalted pistachios, called for in some recipes, are available in large supermarkets.

Polenta

Polenta is a type of meal ground from sweet corn or maize. Used to make a thick Italian cornmeal porridge, polenta is sold several ways. Traditional polenta is made with a coarse-textured cornmeal and requires at least thirty minutes of cooking, with constant stirring. Instant (precooked) polenta has a finer texture and takes far less time.

Pomegranates

Harvested in the autumn, pomegranates have a tangy sweet flavor and are loaded with ruby-red seeds within a bitter white pith and membrane. Choose large pomegranates that are heavy for their size, without blemishes. To harvest the seeds, score the skin from top to bottom into four quarters. Be careful not to puncture the fruit inside, in order to maintain the integrity of the seeds and to avoid a mess. Separate the quarters and remove the red seeds from the white membranes. If you hold the quarters over a bowl and tap a wooden spoon on the back of each one, the seeds come right out, and your hands are still clean. You can also remove the seeds in a bowl of cold water. Pomegranate seeds are a beautiful accent for everything from salads to game roasts.

Potatoes

The ultimate comfort food, potatoes come in many different colors and textures. Here are a few of my favorites:

- *Fingerlings or baby Dutch* potatoes are delicious roasted whole, with a bit of olive oil, at high heat until they are creamy on the inside and browned and crisp on the exterior.
- *Red and white* potatoes, with a waxy texture, are good for roasting and in stews because they keep their texture. They are also delicious as mashed potatoes, although they are not quite as creamy as Yukon Golds or Yellow Finns.
- *Russets* (sometimes called Idahos), with a starchy texture, are good for baking and in gratins because they soak up liquid and become creamy.
- *Yukon Golds and Yellow Finns* are great in just about any potato preparation. They have a rich flavor and consistency.

Port

Port is a sweet fortified wine, with an alcohol content of from 18 to 20 percent. First produced in Portugal (and the best ports still are), port ranges in quality from expensive vintage ports to the lowest-grade ruby ports. In the middle are tawny ports, blends of grapes from several vintages that are aged in wood longer than ruby ports.

Rice vinegar

Chinese and Japanese rice vinegars are milder and sweeter than regular distilled vinegars. They range in color from clear to golden to amber brown, and are also available seasoned or sweetened with sugar. Asian markets and supermarkets sell rice vinegar; once the bottle is opened, the vinegar will keep for several months but will lose flavor and intensity over time.

Ricotta cheese

Smooth and milky tasting, ricotta is an Italian fresh unripened cheese made from the whey of cow's milk or sheep's milk, depending on the region. A low-fat variety is also available.

Serrano chile

Just over one inch long and very slender, serranos pack a lot of punch for their size. The bright green chiles turn red as they ripen and are very hot. When working with chiles, always wear rubber gloves, and wash the cutting surface and knife immediately afterward.

Sesame oil

Sesame oil is rich and dark amber colored, and it tastes like toasted sesame seeds. Sesame oil is used in small amounts to add a nutty flavor and aroma to dressings, marinades, and stir-fries. Don't confuse toasted sesame oil with the clear-pressed sesame seed oil sold in health food stores.

Sun-dried tomatoes

Drying tomatoes greatly intensifies their flavor and gives them a chewy texture. Sun-dried tomatoes are available packaged dried or packed in oil in bottles.

Tomatillo

Tomatillos, which resemble small green tomatoes, are tightly covered in a thin papery husk that needs to be removed before using. Tomatillos are used while they are still firm and green. Popular in Mexican and Southwestern cooking, they are available fresh and canned in Latin markets and large supermarkets.

White balsamic vinegar

Unlike traditional balsamics, this vinegar is produced by simply adding cooked-down grape juice to ordinary white wine vinegar, which gives it an amber color and slightly sweet flavor. While it is not a true balsamic vinegar, it has its place in the pantry. I use it in salad dressings and sauces.

Winter squash

Winter squashes vary in size, shape, and color but they all (except for spaghetti squash) have in common a golden, velvety flesh and a rich, buttery taste. Choose squashes that are heavy for their size and brightly colored. Avoid any with dull shriveled skin, cracks, or bruises. With their thick skin, winter squashes can be a challenge to cut. Use a sharp swivel peeler to remove the hard skin; a sharp knife also works well. Use winter squashes in soups, pie fillings, vegetable gratins, pizza toppings, or as a colorful side dish. They can be braised, roasted, steamed, or even microwaved.

Winter squashes are not for just cooking. Check out the unusual shapes and colors as the season evolves and use them for decoration in centerpieces and as table ornaments at Halloween or Thanksgiving. Put them on your holiday table with pretty fall leaves, votive candles, and pinecones for a festive decoration. Here are a few of my favorite varieties:

- *Acorn* squash resembles a giant acorn; hence its name. Choose the green-colored acorn for its sweet flavor and less stringy flesh.
- *Buttercup* is a dark green, very sweet variety that is more difficult to find; look for it at farmers' markets.
- *Butternut* looks like an elongated bell. Now available year-round, it is great in soups and vegetable gratins, as well as steamed or pureed.
- *Delicata* tastes like a cross between sweet potatoes and butternut squash. It can be used for baking, fillings, gratins, or purees.
- *Hubbard* is a large squash with a bumpy hard skin, ranging in color from dark green to bright orange. It is great for baking and steaming.
- *Kabocha*, a Japanese squash, has the texture of velvet. It is often deep-fried for tempura. I like it to use it in soups.
- *Pumpkins* come in a wide range of sizes. Use large ones for decoration. Small pumpkins, not miniatures, can be used in fillings and soups. The smaller sugar pumpkins, or pie pumpkins, will give you more meat and often a better flavor and texture. Sugar pumpkins make an especially delicious pumpkin soup. Buy an extra one, clean out the cavity, and use it as the soup tureen. Baby pumpkins come in orange and white and make perfect table decorations. You can scoop them out and put votive candles in them.
- *Spaghetti* squash differs from other winter squashes in that the flesh separates into strands when cooked. Select firm, thick-shelled squash. Cut in half and bake or microwave. Flavor the squash "spaghetti" with your favorite pesto.
- *Sweet Dumpling* squash is just the right size for two. Cut it in half and bake it with a bit of maple syrup and butter.

Vanilla extract

Buy only bottles labeled "pure vanilla." I like the bold-flavored Tahitian vanilla, available in gourmet shops and some supermarkets.

BREAKFAST *and* BRUNCH

Cinnamon-Streusel Sour Cream Coffee Cake

Breakfast Polenta with Mascarpone and Maple Syrup

Pumpkin-Chocolate Loaf

Winter Frittata with Sausages, Potatoes, Swiss Chard, and Fontina

Scrambled Eggs with Leeks, Smoked Salmon, and Dill

Holiday Vegetable Strata

Onion, Leek, and Olive Tart

Open-Faced Grilled Cheese and Tomato Sandwiches

Cinnamon-Streusel Sour Cream Coffee Cake

➻ *This moist sour cream coffee cake* is so easy to put together it may become your standby for last-minute brunches. Cinnamon-spiced streusel is a fond childhood taste memory for many of us. Serve this old-fashioned coffee cake for breakfast or brunch, or as an afternoon pick-me-up with a cup of hot tea. I like to put it out on a pretty platter on Christmas morning.

Serves 10 to 12

STREUSEL
1½ cups packed brown sugar
⅓ cup all-purpose flour
1 tablespoon ground cinnamon
Pinch of salt
6 tablespoons (¾ stick) cold unsalted butter

CAKE
3 cups all-purpose flour
1½ teaspoons baking powder
1½ teaspoons baking soda
Pinch of salt
¾ cup (1½ sticks) unsalted butter, softened
1⅓ cups sugar
3 large eggs
1 tablespoon vanilla extract
1 cup sour cream (low-fat is fine)
½ cup milk

1 Preheat the oven to 350°F. Butter and flour a 9-by-13-inch baking pan.

2 *To make the streusel:* In a small bowl, combine the brown sugar, flour, cinnamon, and salt. With your fingers, rub in the butter until the mixture is crumbly. Set aside.

3 *To make the cake:* Sift the flour, baking powder, baking soda, and salt into a medium bowl. In a large bowl, using a hand-held mixer, or in the food processor, cream the butter and sugar until well blended. Add the eggs one at a time and then the vanilla and beat or process until blended. Add the flour mixture alternately with the sour cream and milk and beat or process until just blended.

4 Spread the batter evenly in the prepared pan. Sprinkle the streusel evenly over the top. Bake for about 1 hour, or until a skewer inserted in the center comes out clean.

5 Let the cake cool. Serve cut into large squares.

ADVANCE PREPARATION
This may be made up to 2 days ahead, covered well, and kept at room temperature.

Breakfast Polenta with Mascarpone and Maple Syrup

3 cups milk
¾ cup instant polenta
½ cup freshly grated Parmesan cheese

¼ cup mascarpone
¼ cup maple syrup

→ *Like Cream of Wheat,* instant polenta has a slightly rough texture that makes it an ideal full-bodied hot cereal, the perfect breakfast on a chilly day. The topping of rich mascarpone cheese and sweet maple syrup nicely complements the Parmesan-flavored polenta. Serve this with crisp bacon or sausages for a hearty start to your day.

Serves 4

1 In a medium saucepan, bring the milk to a boil over medium-high heat. Add the polenta and stir constantly with a wooden spoon for about 3 minutes, or until the mixture is slightly thickened. Reduce the heat to medium-low (so that the mixture will not thicken too much before the polenta is cooked through), add the Parmesan cheese, and stir to blend well. Cook, stirring, for another minute.

2 Spoon into cereal bowls and top with the mascarpone and maple syrup. Serve immediately.

Pumpkin-Chocolate Loaf

→ **Peet's,** a California coffee store, serves slices of its pumpkin-chocolate bread along with brimming cups of hot coffee. My first taste of this tea bread surprised me with just how well the flavors of chocolate and pumpkin went together. When I re-created the recipe, I increased the amount of chocolate and swirled it through the pumpkin batter, using a skewer to streak the melted chocolate.

Serve this for breakfast or for afternoon tea, or for dessert with sliced ripe pears. This is also the basis for Pumpkin-Chocolate Bread Pudding (page 151). Since the recipe doubles easily, make two loaves and stick one in the freezer so you can prepare the bread pudding later.

Serves 12

1¾ cups all-purpose flour
1 teaspoon baking powder
1 teaspoon baking soda
1½ teaspoons pumpkin pie spice
½ teaspoon salt
½ cup (1 stick) unsalted butter, softened

1¼ cups sugar
3 large eggs
1 cup canned pumpkin puree
1 teaspoon vanilla extract
4 ounces semisweet or bittersweet chocolate, cut into pieces

1 Preheat the oven to 350°F. Butter and flour a 9-by-5-inch nonstick loaf pan.

2 In a medium mixing bowl, combine the flour, baking powder, baking soda, pumpkin pie spice, and salt and whisk together.

3 In a large bowl, with an electric mixer, beat the butter until creamy. Add the sugar and continue beating until light and fluffy. Add the eggs one at a time and beat until well blended. Add the pumpkin puree and vanilla, then add the flour mixture, beating just until well blended.

4 In the top of a double boiler, melt the chocolate over medium-high heat, stirring occasionally until smooth, about 5 minutes. Or melt in a glass bowl in the microwave for 1½ to 2 minutes, until completely melted and smooth.

5 Spoon half of the batter into the loaf pan. Spoon half of the melted chocolate on top of the batter and swirl it into the batter with a wooden skewer. Repeat with the remaining batter and chocolate, making sure to swirl the chocolate into the batter well.

6 Bake the loaf for about 1 hour, or until a metal skewer inserted in the center comes out clean. Let the loaf cool for 15 minutes on a wire rack, then invert onto the rack and turn right-side up. Serve warm or at room temperature, cut into slices.

ADVANCE PREPARATION
This may be made up to 1 day ahead, covered tightly, and kept at room temperature.

Winter Frittata with Sausages, Potatoes, Swiss Chard, and Fontina

3 tablespoons olive oil

4 favorite cooked sausages (about
1 pound), sliced into 1-inch pieces

1 medium leek, white and light green parts
only, cleaned and finely chopped

1 pound red or white waxy potatoes,
peeled and cut into 1/2-inch dice

1 small bunch Swiss chard (about
1/2 pound), stems removed and leaves
torn into small pieces

Salt and freshly ground black pepper

12 large eggs

2 tablespoons finely chopped fresh parsley

1 1/2 cups shredded Italian Fontina cheese

GARNISH

1/4 cup sour cream

1/4 cup favorite fresh tomato salsa or
Salsa Verde (page 162)

➜ *Frittatas are incredibly versatile* because you can fill them with so many things. And, easier to master than a regular rolled omelet, they can be served hot or warm or be prepared ahead and served at room temperature. The hearty combination of ingredients in this version makes it a meal in one dish. Serve with a simple mixed fruit salad for a satisfying breakfast or brunch. Try it with crispy bacon instead of sausages, or with cherry tomatoes or yellow cheddar cheese for a colorful alternative.

Serves 6

1 Preheat the oven to 350°F. In a 10-inch nonstick skillet with an ovenproof handle (cover the handle with foil if not oven proof), heat 1 tablespoon of the oil over medium-high heat. Add the sausages and sauté for about 4 minutes, until nicely browned. Remove the sausages with a slotted spoon and drain on paper towels.

2 Add the remaining 2 tablespoons oil to the pan and reduce the heat to medium. Add the leek and potatoes and sauté for about 20 minutes, stirring frequently, until the leek is golden brown and the potatoes are tender inside and crisp on the surface. Stir in the chard, cover, and cook for about 2 minutes, until the chard is wilted. Season with salt and pepper.

3 Meanwhile, combine the eggs, parsley, and salt and pepper to taste in a medium bowl and whisk until well blended. Stir in 1 1/4 cups of the shredded cheese.

4 Add the sausages to the potato mixture and spread the mixture evenly in the skillet. Pour the egg mixture over it and cook over medium-low heat, stirring occasionally, for about 7 minutes, until the bottom is lightly set and cooked. Sprinkle with the remaining 1/4 cup cheese.

5 Transfer the skillet to the oven and bake for 10 to 15 minutes, or until the frittata is puffed and brown. Serve right in the pan, or slide onto a round serving platter. Garnish with the sour cream and salsa, and serve immediately.

ADVANCE PREPARATION

This may be prepared up to 8 hours ahead, covered, and refrigerated. Bring to room temperature before serving.

Scrambled Eggs with Leeks, Smoked Salmon, and Dill

3 tablespoons unsalted butter

1 tablespoon olive oil

3 leeks, white and light green parts only, cleaned and finely chopped

Salt and freshly ground black pepper

12 large eggs

¼ cup heavy (whipping) cream

¼ pound sliced smoked salmon, diced

1 tablespoon finely chopped fresh dill weed for garnish

➜ *This take on lox, onions, and eggs* turns a casual breakfast into a special occasion. I like to use Nova, but you can choose your favorite smoked salmon. Mixing it in at the end of cooking the eggs ensures that the salmon stays tender. Serve these elegant scrambled eggs with warm Cinnamon-Streusel Sour Cream Coffee Cake (page 20), a platter of fresh oranges, and bowls of café au lait. If you're cooking for a crowd, this recipe doubles easily; use a very large deep sauté pan to accommodate all the ingredients.

Serves 4

1 In a large skillet, melt 2 tablespoons of the butter with the oil over medium heat. Add the leeks and sauté, stirring occasionally, for about 10 minutes, or until they are golden brown and very tender. Season with salt and pepper. Set aside.

2 In a medium bowl, whisk the eggs well to combine. Put a fine strainer over another bowl and strain the eggs, leaving the albumen (the white stringy part) in the strainer. Add the cream and salt and pepper to taste to the eggs and stir to combine.

3 In a large deep skillet, melt the remaining 1 tablespoon butter over medium heat. Add the eggs and cook, stirring constantly with a wooden spoon, until they begin to set. Keep stirring for about 3 more minutes, or until the eggs are very creamy. Add the leeks and salmon and cook for 2 to 3 more minutes, until they are heated through but the eggs are still creamy, not dry. Turn into a shallow bowl and garnish with the dill. Serve immediately.

Holiday Vegetable Strata

→ *This savory pudding* has become a tradition around our house: the holiday buffet wouldn't be the same without a big square of it on the table. Strata is a layered bread pudding (its name means "layers" in Italian) that can include a variety of ingredients. Feel free to put your own signature on it with the addition of sausage or prosciutto, roasted red peppers, or other cooked vegetables.

The strata is best assembled the night before cooking in order for the bread to absorb the custard, making it perfect for entertaining a crowd. Then all you have to do on the day of your party is put the strata in the oven an hour before your guests arrive. I prefer to use an egg bread like challah for its rich flavor. Buy the bread two days ahead so there is time for it to dry out. I also like to serve a fresh fruit salad with this dish. Start with sparkling wine mixed with blood orange juice, and let the fun begin.

Serves 6 to 8

2 tablespoons olive oil
2 leeks, white and light green parts only, cleaned and finely chopped
¾ pound cremini mushrooms, sliced
Salt and freshly ground black pepper
One 14-ounce loaf egg bread, crusts removed, cut into cubes, and dried out for at least a day on a baking sheet at room temperature

2 cups torn spinach leaves
2 cups shredded cheddar cheese
4 large eggs
3½ cups milk
¼ cup finely chopped fresh parsley
2 teaspoons whole-grain mustard
2 tablespoons freshly grated Parmesan cheese

1 In a large skillet, heat the oil over medium heat. Add the leeks and sauté for about 5 minutes, or until softened and lightly browned. Add the mushrooms and cook, stirring occasionally, for about 5 more minutes, until tender. Season with salt and pepper and set aside.

2 Place half of the bread in a greased 9-by-13-inch baking dish. Spoon the mushroom-leek mixture evenly over the bread and scatter the spinach evenly over the top. Sprinkle on 1 cup of the cheddar cheese. Place the remaining bread on top.

3 In a large bowl, combine the eggs, milk, parsley, mustard, the remaining 1 cup cheese, and salt and pepper to taste. Whisk to blend well. Carefully pour the mixture evenly over the bread. Sprinkle with the Parmesan cheese. Cover tightly with foil and refrigerate overnight.

4 An hour before you are ready to bake, remove the strata from the refrigerator. Preheat the oven to 350°F. Bake the strata for 45 to 50 minutes, or until slightly puffed, set, and browned on the top. Let rest for a few minutes, then cut into pieces and serve. Or let cool and serve slightly warm or at room temperature.

ADVANCE PREPARATION
This must be made through Step 3 the night before serving.

Onion, Leek, and Olive Tart

→ *Layers of flavor* give this savory tart its signature. A sweet jam-like onion mixture is combined with a cheese custard accented with sun-dried tomatoes and olives, and the result is simply sublime. If you are in a hurry, use a packaged store-bought crust. I like to serve this alongside a mixed green salad as a main course for brunch. Small slices of the tart are also good as a first course.

Serves 8

FILLING

3 tablespoons olive oil

1 tablespoon unsalted butter

2 large yellow onions, very thinly sliced

4 large leeks, white and light green parts only, cleaned and thinly sliced

½ teaspoon sugar

Salt and freshly ground black pepper

3 large eggs

¾ cup milk

2 tablespoons Sun-Dried Tomato Pesto (page 159)

½ cup pitted and chopped Kalamata olives

½ cup, plus 3 tablespoons shredded Gruyère cheese

PASTRY

1 cup all-purpose flour

Pinch of salt

6 tablespoons (¾ stick) chilled unsalted butter cut into small pieces

About ¼ cup ice water

2 tablespoons Dijon mustard

2 tablespoons freshly grated Parmesan cheese

1 *To make the filling:* In a very large deep sauté pan, heat the oil and butter over medium-high heat. Add the onions, leeks, sugar, and salt and pepper to taste and toss with tongs to coat the vegetables evenly. Sauté for about 30 to 35 minutes, or until the onions and leeks are browned and caramelized and almost resemble marmalade; stir constantly toward the end of the cooking time to brown the onions evenly. (If the onions begin to stick and seem too brown, add ¼ cup water and scrape up the brown bits before continuing.) Taste for seasoning. Let cool.

2 Meanwhile, preheat the oven to 375°F.

3 *To make the pastry:* Combine the flour and salt in a food processor and process for a few seconds to blend. Add the butter and process until the mixture resembles coarse meal, 5 to 10 seconds. With the blades turning, gradually add the water until the dough is just beginning to come together and will adhere when pinched.

4 Transfer the dough to a floured pastry board or work surface and shape into a disk for easy rolling. Roll out into a 13-inch circle. Drape the circle over the rolling pin and fit it into an 11-inch tart pan with removable bottom. Roll the pin over the tart pan with moderate pressure to remove any excess overhanging dough. Place the tart pan on a baking sheet.

5 Prick the shell all over and line it with a large piece of parchment or wax paper. Fill with dried beans or baking beads to prevent the shell from shrinking. Bake for about 22 minutes, or until very light brown. Remove from the oven. Leave the oven on.

CONTINUED

Onion, Leek, and Olive Tart

6 Remove the paper and beans, and brush the shell with the mustard. Sprinkle on the Parmesan cheese. Place the shell back in the oven for about 7 minutes, or until the cheese is melted. Reduce the oven temperature to 350°F.

7 While the cheese melts, beat the eggs, milk, pesto, olives, and ½ cup of the Gruyère in a bowl until well blended. Spread the onion mixture evenly in the tart shell. Spoon the custard mixture evenly over the onion mixture and sprinkle with the remaining 3 table-spoons Gruyère.

8 Bake the tart for 30 to 35 minutes, or until the cheese on top is melted and the filling does not jiggle when gently shaken. Serve hot, warm, or at room temperature.

9 To serve: remove the sides of the tart pan and place the tart on a serving dish. Slice into wedges.

ADVANCE PREPARATION

The tart is best eaten the day it is baked, but it may be made through Step 3 up to 1 day ahead. Cover the unbaked tart shell and chill filling serarately and refrigerate. Bring the filling to room temperature before filling the baked shell.

Open-Faced Grilled Cheese and Tomato Sandwiches

→ *These sophisticated grilled cheese* sandwiches are an adaptation of the Welsh rarebit served at Balthazar restaurant in New York City. Sure to hit the spot on a rainy day, you could add some crumbled crispy bacon to the cheese mixture if you like. Serve with a bowl of Ribollita (page 43) for a satisfying brunch or casual supper.

Serves 4

¾ pound sharp cheddar cheese, shredded
2 teaspoons whole-grain mustard
2 large egg yolks
¼ cup beer
1 teaspoon Worcestershire sauce

Salt and freshly ground black pepper
4 slices Roma (plum) tomatoes
1 teaspoon olive oil
4 large slices sourdough bread

1 Preheat the broiler. In a medium bowl, combine the cheese, mustard, egg yolks, beer, and Worcestershire sauce, and season with salt and pepper, stirring until blended.

2 Place the tomato slices on a small baking sheet. Brush with the oil and season with salt and pepper. Broil until they are beginning to brown and are bubbling. Set aside.

3 Place the bread on another small baking sheet and toast under the broiler until lightly browned on top. Remove from the broiler and spread the cheese mixture over the toast. Broil until the cheese is bubbly and melted. Place each sandwich on a plate and arrange a broiled tomato slice on top. Serve immediately.

ADVANCE PREPARATION
This may be prepared through Step 1 up to 1 day ahead, covered, and refrigerated.

Belgian Endive Salad with Apples, Toasted Walnuts, and Fig Vinaigrette

Grapefruit, Mushroom, and Avocado Salad

Autumn Salad with Persimmons and Pomegranates

Frisée Salad with Bacon and Goat Cheese

Marinated Roasted Beets with Orange-Balsamic Vinaigrette

Sliced Fennel Salad with Lemon Parmesan Dressing

SALADS *and* SOUPS

Ribollita

French Onion and Fennel Soup

Fire-Roasted Tomato and Eggplant Bisque

Hearty Lentil Soup with Grilled Sweet and Hot Italian Sausages

Mushroom Soup with Port

Chicken Soup with Matzo Balls

Butternut Squash and Chestnut Soup with Chipotle Cream

Belgian Endive Salad with Apples, Toasted Walnuts, and Fig Vinaigrette

→ *This is wonderful* as a cold-weather first-course salad. Crisp apple slices sweeten Belgian endive and toasted walnuts. Dried figs add a fruity richness to the vinaigrette. Follow the salad with Short Ribs with Dried Mushrooms and Fire-Roasted Tomatoes (page 74) and Roasted Jerusalem Artichokes and Carrots (page 127).

Serves 6

1 cup coarsely chopped walnuts
10 Belgian endive, cores removed and sliced lengthwise into thin strips
2 Fuji or Pink Lady apples, peeled, cored, and cut into thin strips

DRESSING
1 teaspoon Dijon mustard
2 tablespoons red wine vinegar
1 tablespoon white balsamic vinegar
Salt and freshly ground black pepper
½ cup olive oil
½ cup dried figs, finely chopped

1 Heat a small skillet over medium-low heat. Add the walnuts and toss gently for about 2 to 3 minutes, until they begin to brown lightly and become fragrant. Remove from the heat.

2 In a salad bowl, combine the endive and apple strips. Sprinkle over the walnuts.

3 *To make the dressing:* In a small bowl, whisk together the mustard and vinegars, and season with salt and pepper. Whisking constantly, slowly add the oil until incorporated. Stir in the figs. Taste for seasoning.

4 Pour the dressing over the salad and toss to coat well. Serve on salad plates.

ADVANCE PREPARATION
This may be made up to 2 hours ahead through Step 3. Make sure to cover the salad tightly with plastic wrap so the apples won't turn brown, and refrigerate. Leave the dressing, covered, at room temperature.

Grapefruit, Mushroom, and Avocado Salad

→ **This salad celebrates** winter's bounty. The grapefruit juice in the vinaigrette intensifies the citrus flavor. Serve before Hearty Lentil Soup with Grilled Sweet and Hot Italian Sausages (page 46), with a basket of warm sourdough bread. Or for an elegant dinner, start with this and continue with Crispy Roast Duck with Lavender Honey Sauce (page 69) and Autumn Noodles and Rice (page 111).

Serves 4 to 6

DRESSING
1 medium shallot, finely chopped
Juice of 1/2 pink grapefruit
1 tablespoon balsamic vinegar
1/2 cup olive oil
Salt and freshly ground black pepper

2 medium heads butter lettuce, torn into
   bite-sized pieces
1 large pink grapefruit, peeled, sectioned,
   and cut into 1-inch pieces
4 medium white mushrooms, thinly sliced
1 ripe avocado, peeled, pitted, and sliced

1 *To make the dressing:* In a small bowl, combine the shallot, grapefruit juice, and vinegar. Slowly add the oil, whisking until completely incorporated. Season with salt and pepper.

2 Place the lettuce in a shallow salad bowl. Arrange the grapefruit, mushrooms, and avocado slices on top of the lettuce in an attractive pattern.

3 Bring the salad to the table, toss with dressing, and serve.

ADVANCE PREPARATION
The salad may be made up to 2 hours ahead through Step 2, without the avocado, covered, and refrigerated. Add the avocado just before serving. Leave the dressing, covered, at room temperature.

Autumn Salad with Persimmons and Pomegranates

➜ *A salute to autumn's finest,* this colorful salad combines fresh greens and endive with the accents of vibrant orange persimmons and garnet-red pomegranate seeds. This is an elegant first course or side dish on a larger buffet, and the recipe can easily be doubled or tripled.

Serves 4 to 6

¼ pound mixed salad greens
8 Belgian endive, cores removed and thinly sliced crosswise
3 medium Fuyu persimmons, peeled and sliced
Seeds from 1 medium pomegranate (about ¾ cup)
¼ pound soft fresh goat cheese, crumbled

DRESSING
2 tablespoons sherry vinegar
1 tablespoon white balsamic vinegar
Salt and freshly ground black pepper
6 tablespoons olive oil

1 Place the greens and endive in a large salad bowl. Scatter the persimmon slices, pomegranate seeds, and goat cheese on top. Set aside.

2 *To make the dressing:* In a small bowl, combine the vinegars and season with salt and pepper. Slowly add the oil, whisking constantly until incorporated. Taste for seasoning.

3 Pour the dressing over the salad and toss to coat. Serve immediately.

ADVANCE PREPARATION
The salad can be assembled up to 4 hours ahead, covered, and refrigerated. Remove from the refrigerator 30 minutes before serving. The dressing can also be made ahead and left, covered, at room temperature.

Frisée Salad with Bacon and Goat Cheese

2 tablespoons olive oil
1/4 cup French-bread bread crumbs or
  panko (Japanese bread crumbs)
1/2 pound fresh goat cheese log
2 heads frisée lettuce (curly endive), cored,
  and leaves torn into 3-inch pieces

3/4 pound thick-sliced bacon, cut
  into 1/2-inch-wide pieces
2 shallots, finely chopped
5 tablespoons red wine vinegar
Salt and freshly ground black pepper

→ *This classic French bistro salad* is a favorite of mine as a main course for lunch or a first course for dinner. Although sometimes confused with escarole, which has broad leaves, frisée, or curly endive, has distinctive frilly, slightly bitter leaves. Instead of the traditional croutons, I like slices of warm goat cheese, coated in bread crumbs and baked until crunchy outside and creamy within. If you're in the mood for soup and salad, serve this with a bowl of Ribollita (page 43).

Serves 4 to 6

1 Spoon the oil into a small bowl, and put the bread crumbs in another small bowl. Cut the cheese into 4 equal disks. With tongs, dip the cheese into the olive oil, then roll in the bread crumbs, and put in a shallow baking dish. Cover and refrigerate for at least 1 hour.

2 Shortly before serving, preheat the oven to 450°F. Bake the goat cheese for 10 minutes, or until the crumbs are brown and the inside is soft.

3 Meanwhile, place the frisée in a large salad bowl.

4 In a large skillet, cook the bacon over medium-high heat, stirring occasionally, for about 4 to 5 minutes until crisp. With a slotted spoon, remove the bacon and drain on paper towels. Add the shallots to the pan and sauté for 1 minute, or until softened. Add the red wine vinegar, reduce the heat to medium, and simmer for 1 minute, or until slightly reduced. Season with salt and pepper.

5 Pour the warm dressing over the salad greens, add the bacon, and toss to coat evenly. Divide the greens among salad bowls, making sure there is an even amount of bacon in each salad. Place the goat cheese on top and serve immediately.

ADVANCE PREPARATION
The cheese may be breaded up to 6 hours ahead, covered, and refrigerated.

Marinated Roasted Beets with Orange-Balsamic Vinaigrette

➜ *These rosy beets* are accented with an orange-flavored vinaigrette and toasted pecans; walnuts also work well. I like to serve this on a bed of bright green arugula sprinkled with crumbled feta cheese for a beautiful color contrast. Take this on a tailgate picnic, or serve it as a first course.

Serves 6

2 medium bunches beets (about 2 pounds), trimmed and scrubbed
¼ cup coarsely chopped pecans

DRESSING
2 tablespoons orange juice
1 tablespoon balsamic vinegar
1 teaspoon Dijon mustard

¼ cup olive oil
Salt and freshly ground black pepper
2 tablespoon chopped fresh chives

1 bunch arugula, trimmed and cleaned
1 tablespoon finely chopped fresh parsley for garnish

1 Preheat the oven to 425°F. Place the beets in a roasting pan and add ¼ inch of water. Cover the pan with foil and roast for 45 minutes, or until the beets are fork-tender. Let cool slightly. Reduce the oven temperature to 350°F.

2 Place the nuts on a baking sheet and toast for 5 to 7 minutes, or until lightly browned and aromatic. Set aside.

3 When they are cool enough to handle, peel the beets and cut into ½-inch pieces. Transfer to a bowl, cover, and refrigerate.

4 *To make the dressing:* In a small bowl, combine the orange juice, vinegar, and mustard and whisk to blend. Gradually add the olive oil, whisking until blended. Season with salt and pepper, and add the chives. Taste for seasoning.

5 Pour the dressing over the beets and toss to coat evenly.

6 To serve, sprinkle the nuts over the beets. Arrange a bed of arugula on each serving plate, and place the beets on top. Garnish with the parsley.

ADVANCE PREPARATION
This may be made through Step 5 up to 1 day ahead, covered, and refrigerated.

Sliced Fennel Salad with Lemon Parmesan Dressing

→ *I used to serve fennel* with a traditional white wine vinaigrette, but when I experimented with fresh lemon juice instead, I was happily surprised. Grated Parmesan is added to the dressing, and then the salad is garnished with shards of the same cheese: not only delicious, but eye appealing as well. Serve this as a starter before Veal Ragù on Pappardelle (page 86) or Rosemary-Orange Glazed Chicken (page 54).

Serves 4 to 6

4 fennel bulbs (about 2 pounds)

DRESSING
2 garlic cloves, minced
¼ cup fresh lemon juice
¼ cup chopped fennel fronds (from above)
2 tablespoons finely sliced fresh chives

Salt and freshly ground black pepper
½ cup olive oil
2 tablespoons finely grated Parmesan cheese

A 1-ounce wedge of Parmesan cheese

1 Trim the stalks and fronds from the fennel; reserve enough fronds to make ¼ cup chopped. Cut the bulbs lengthwise into quarters and trim away the core at the base. Thinly slice the fennel. Chop the reserved fronds.

2 *To make the dressing:* In a large bowl, whisk together the garlic, lemon juice, fennel fronds, and chives, and season with salt and pepper. Whisking constantly, slowly add the olive oil until incorporated. Add the grated cheese. Taste for seasoning.

3 Add the fennel to the dressing and stir to coat. Arrange on a platter or serving plates. Using a swivel vegetable peeler, shave large shards of Parmesan over the top of the salads. Serve immediately.

ADVANCE PREPARATION
The salad may be prepared up to 2 hours ahead, covered and refrigerated. Shave the Parmesan at the last minute.

Ribollita

→ *In Italian the word* ribollita translates as "reboiled," or twice-cooked. This
make-ahead vegetarian soup is note-
worthy for its rustic texture. A simple white
bean stock is enriched with a variety of
greens and tomatoes, slices of toasted
bread are added, and the soup is refrigerated overnight. The next day, all you have
to do is "reboil" the soup and serve with
a drizzle of olive oil and a sprinkling of
aged Parmesan cheese.

Serves 8

1 pound dried cannellini beans
12 cups water
3 garlic cloves, peeled
5 fresh sage leaves
1/2 cup fruity olive oil
2 onions, coarsely chopped
3 carrots, peeled and sliced
3 stalks celery, sliced
1 medium eggplant, peeled and cut
into 1/2-inch pieces
2 medium russet (baking) potatoes,
peeled and thickly sliced

1/2 small Savoy cabbage, cored and
coarsely chopped
1 bunch red Swiss chard, trimmed and
coarsely chopped
1 bunch kale, trimmed and coarsely chopped
One 14 1/2-ounce can crushed tomatoes
Salt and freshly ground black pepper
12 slices French bread, toasted
Freshly grated Parmesan cheese for serving
Olive oil for serving

1 In a large bowl, cover the beans with cold water and soak overnight; drain. Or, if you
prefer to do a quick-soak method, in a large saucepan, combine the beans and water to
cover, bring to a boil, and cook for 2 minutes. Remove from the heat, cover, and let stand
for 1 hour; drain.

2 In a very large soup pot, combine the beans, 12 cups water, garlic, and sage and bring
to a simmer over medium-high heat. Reduce the heat to low and simmer for 1 1/2 to 2 hours,
or until the beans are tender. Let cool.

3 Remove 1 cup of the beans and reserve. With a hand blender, puree the remaining
beans in the cooking liquid. Or puree in batches in a regular blender. Transfer to a large
bowl and set aside.

4 Rinse out and dry the pot. Add 1/4 cup of the oil and heat over medium heat. Add the
onions and sauté for 10 to 12 minutes, or until softened and slightly browned. Add the
carrots, celery, eggplant, potatoes, cabbage, chard, and kale, tossing the vegetables to coat
them evenly. Add the tomatoes, season with salt and pepper, cover, and cook for about 20
minutes, or until the greens have wilted. (Toss them a few times to encourage even cooking.)

5 Add the pureed beans and cook, covered, for another 40 minutes, or until the soup is
nicely thickened. Add the reserved beans and taste for seasoning. Add the toasted bread
and cook for another 10 minutes, or until it is soaked through. Let cool, cover, and refrigerate overnight.

6 Shortly before serving, reheat the soup over low heat for about 20 minutes, or until
bubbling. Taste for seasoning.

7 To serve, ladle the soup into soup bowls. Grate cheese over each bowl and drizzle a
tablespoon or so of the remaining olive oil over each serving.

ADVANCE PREPARATION
This must be made through Step 5 a day ahead.

French Onion and Fennel Soup

→ *French onion soup* (see photograph, page 168) is one of my all-time favorites. Although I don't like to mess with perfection, this adaptation is equally tasty. Fennel infuses the onion with a subtle anise flavor. Slowly caramelizing the onions and fennel takes awhile, so I like to make this over the weekend and then serve it on a weeknight, since it just takes a few minutes to reheat. Serve with a simple salad of Belgian endive with a mustard vinaigrette.

Serves 4 to 6

3 tablespoons olive oil
8 large yellow onions, thinly sliced
3 fennel bulbs (about 1½ pounds), trimmed, cored, and thinly sliced
¼ teaspoon sugar
7 cups chicken or beef broth
½ cup dry white wine
6 medium garlic cloves, minced

1 bay leaf
¼ teaspoon dried thyme
Salt and freshly ground black pepper
Twelve ¼-inch-thick slices French bread
¾ cup shredded Gruyère cheese
2 tablespoons finely chopped fresh parsley for garnish

1 In a large nonaluminum Dutch oven or soup pot, heat the oil over medium heat. Add the onions and sauté, tossing and turning frequently, for about 15 minutes, until lightly browned.

2 Add the fennel and sugar and cook, stirring frequently, for about 30 to 45 more minutes, until the vegetables are caramelized.

3 Add the broth, white wine, garlic, bay leaf, and thyme. Partially cover and simmer for 30 minutes. Season with salt and pepper, and discard the bay leaf. Remove from the heat.

4 Preheat the broiler. Broil the bread for about 1½ to 2 minutes on each side, or until golden, watching carefully to prevent burning.

5 Ladle the soup into ovenproof soup bowls. Place 2 or 3 toasts on top of each and sprinkle evenly with the cheese. Broil until the cheese is golden brown. Sprinkle a little chopped parsley over each soup bowl, and serve immediately.

ADVANCE PREPARATION
This may be prepared through Step 3 up to 3 days ahead, covered, and refrigerated. Reheat gently. This soup also freezes well. Adjust the seasonings when you reheat the soup.

Fire-Roasted Tomato and Eggplant Bisque

The thought of tomato soup always evokes warm memories. On rainy days, my grandmother would pick me up from nursery school and take me home for a bowl of creamy tomato soup and an egg salad sandwich. This is an update of that taste memory. The fire-roasted tomatoes add a light smoky flavor, and the eggplant thickens the soup. Serve this with Open-Faced Grilled Cheese and Tomato Sandwiches (page 31) for Saturday lunch or a light supper.

Serves 6

¼ cup olive oil
1 medium onion, finely chopped
1 medium carrot, finely chopped
1 stalk celery, finely chopped
½ medium purple eggplant or 3 Japanese eggplant, peeled and diced
Salt
2 garlic cloves, minced
2 tablespoons all-purpose flour

Two 14½-ounce cans fire-roasted diced tomatoes, with their juice
¼ cup tomato paste
1 teaspoon sugar
3 cups chicken or vegetable broth
1 tablespoon balsamic vinegar
1 cup milk or half-and-half
White pepper
½ cup croutons, preferably cheese or garlic, for garnish

1 In a medium soup pot, heat the oil over medium heat. Add the onion, carrot, and celery and cook for 4 to 5 minutes, or until the vegetables begin to soften. Add the eggplant and a pinch of salt and sauté for 5 minutes, or until the eggplant is very soft. Add the garlic and cook for 1 minute, or until slightly softened.

2 Reduce the heat to low, sprinkle the flour over the vegetables, stirring constantly, and cook, for 2 minutes, or until the flour is incorporated into the vegetables and thickened. Add the tomatoes, tomato paste, sugar, and broth and bring to a simmer over medium-high heat. Partially cover the pot, reduce the heat to medium, and cook, stirring occasionally, for 15 minutes, or until the vegetables are cooked and all the flavors are well blended. Remove from the heat.

3 With a hand blender, blend the soup until it is roughly pureed, with some texture remaining. Or transfer to a regular blender, in batches, and roughly puree; return to the pot. Add the vinegar, return the soup to medium heat, and cook for 2 minutes. Add the milk, stirring to combine, and cook for another minute. Season with salt and pepper.

4 To serve, ladle the soup into soup bowls and garnish with the croutons.

ADVANCE PREPARATION
The soup may be made up to 2 days ahead, covered, and refrigerated. Reheat gently, and season to taste.

Hearty Lentil Soup with Grilled Sweet and Hot Italian Sausages

I like to use brown lentils for this terrific soup because they cook quickly and puree well. The grilled sweet and hot sausages make it a substantial dish. A loaf of crusty bread is all that is needed for a simple all-in-one meal. Serve for Sunday supper or a chilly wintry afternoon's lunch.

Serves 8

2 tablespoons olive oil
1 large onion, finely chopped
3 carrots, peeled and finely chopped
2 stalks celery, finely chopped
3 garlic cloves, minced
2 cups brown lentils, rinsed and picked over
8 cups chicken broth, or as needed
One 14½-ounce can diced tomatoes
¼ cup finely chopped fresh parsley, plus 2 tablespoons for garnish
1 bay leaf
½ teaspoon dried thyme
1 pound sweet Italian sausage
1 pound hot Italian sausage
1 tablespoon balsamic vinegar
Salt and freshly ground black pepper

1 In a large soup pot, heat the oil over medium heat. Add the onion and sauté for about 3 minutes, or until softened. Add the carrots and celery and sauté for about 5 minutes, or until slightly softened. Add the garlic and sauté for another minute, or until softened.

2 Add the lentils, chicken broth, tomatoes, 2 tablespoons of the parsley, the bay leaf, and thyme and bring to a simmer. Reduce the heat to medium-low and cook, stirring occasionally, for about 30 minutes, or until the lentils are tender. Test for tenderness by pressing on them with the back of a wooden spoon; if they break up easily, they are cooked. Remove the bay leaf.

3 While the soup is cooking, grill the sausages. Heat a nonstick grill pan over medium-high heat. Add the sausages and grill, turning to brown evenly, for about 6 to 8 minutes, or until nicely browned. Let cool, and cut into ½-inch slices. Set aside.

4 Coarsely blend the soup with a hand blender until it is roughly pureed. Or puree the soup in a regular blender in batches, making sure to retain some texture; return it to the pot. If the soup seems too thick, add up to 1 more cup of broth or water to bring it to the desired consistency.

5 Add 2 tablespoons parsley, the vinegar, and season with salt and pepper, then add the sausages. Simmer for 5 more minutes. Taste for seasoning.

6 Ladle into soup bowls and garnish with the remaining 2 tablespoons parsley. Serve immediately.

ADVANCE PREPARATION
The soup may be prepared up to 3 days in advance, covered, and refrigerated. Reheat gently. The soup also freezes well. Adjust the seasonings when you reheat the soup.

Mushroom Soup with Port

➟ *Combining dried wild mushrooms* with brown cremini mushrooms gives this soup extra body as well as a richer flavor. I've found that soy sauce intensifies the mushroom flavor. If you don't have port, you can use sherry. This would be a sophisticated beginning to an elegant dinner party. Follow with Pork Chops with Sweet Cherry Peppers (page 83) and Braised Spinach with Leeks and Roasted Garlic (page 129).

Serves 4

1 ounce dried wild mushrooms, such as
   shiitake or porcini
4 cups chicken or vegetable broth
¼ cup (½ stick) unsalted butter
1 medium onion, finely chopped
¾ pound cremini mushrooms, thinly sliced
3 tablespoons all-purpose flour

Salt and white pepper
2 teaspoons soy sauce
1 cup half-and-half
5 tablespoons tawny port or dry sherry
2 tablespoons finely chopped fresh parsley
   for garnish

1 In a medium saucepan, combine the dried mushrooms and broth and bring to a boil. Cover and simmer for 5 minutes. Lift the mushrooms out of the pan. Strain the broth into a bowl and add the mushrooms to the broth. Set aside.

2 In a medium soup pot, melt the butter over medium heat. Add the onion and sauté, stirring occasionally, for 3 minutes, or until soft. Add the cremini mushrooms and sauté for another 3 minutes, or until softened. Sprinkle with the flour and salt and pepper. Stir for 1 minute to cook the flour and coat the mushrooms. Whisk in the strained broth, with the mushrooms, add the soy sauce, and simmer for 15 minutes, partially covered.

3 With a hand blender, blend the soup until it is roughly pureed, with some texture remaining. Or transfer to a regular blender, in batches, and roughly puree; return to the pot. Add the half-and-half and port, bring to a simmer, and simmer for 2 minutes, or until the alcohol has burned off. Taste for seasoning.

4 To serve, ladle into soup bowls and garnish with the chopped parsley.

ADVANCE PREPARATION
The soup may be made up to 1 day ahead, covered, and refrigerated. Reheat gently, and adjust the seasonings.

Chicken Soup with Matzo Balls

→ *Feeling like a cold* or flu may be coming your way? Try this magical potion that some consider to be better than medicine. This is the dish to have on days when you just need a cup of comfort. Serve it as a main dish for lunch or dinner.

The soup is made in two stages: some of the vegetables are used to prepare the chicken broth and then strained out; fresh vegetables are added to the stock and simmered until just cooked through. The two-step process both flavors the soup and results in vegetables that are perfectly cooked. You can purchase schmaltz in the freezer section of the supermarket or make it yourself, or substitute vegetable oil.

Serves 6 to 8

One 4- to 5-pound roasting chicken, cut into serving pieces
4 cups chicken broth
8 cups water
2 medium onions, finely chopped
8 carrots, peeled, 4 cut into $\frac{1}{2}$-inch-thick slices; 4 cut into 3-by-$\frac{1}{2}$-inch-thick strips
3 parsnips, peeled, 1 cut into $\frac{1}{2}$-inch-thick slices; 2 cut into 3-by-$\frac{1}{2}$-inch-thick strips
2 stalks celery, cut into $\frac{1}{2}$-inch-thick slices
1 bunch fresh dill, leaves plucked and coarsely chopped
Salt and freshly ground black pepper

6 leeks, white and light green parts only, cleaned and left whole
3 tablespoons finely chopped fresh parsley

MATZO BALLS
$\frac{1}{4}$ cup rendered chicken fat (schmaltz) or vegetable oil
4 large eggs, lightly beaten
1 cup matzo meal
$1\frac{1}{2}$ teaspoons salt
$\frac{1}{4}$ cup seltzer or other sparkling water

3 tablespoons finely chopped fresh parsley for garnish

1 Place the chicken in a large soup pot, add the broth and water, and bring to a boil over medium-high heat. Skim the soup. Add the onions, sliced carrots, sliced parsnip, celery, and dill. Reduce the heat and simmer for $1\frac{1}{2}$ to 2 hours, or until the chicken is cooked and the soup is full flavored; skim periodically. Season with salt and pepper.

2 Strain the soup through a large strainer into another pot. Remove the chicken and discard the cooked vegetables. Remove the chicken meat from the bones, discarding the skin and any cartilage, and tear the chicken into bite-sized pieces. Cover and refrigerate.

3 Add the leeks and the remaining carrots and parsnips to the soup, adjust the seasoning, and bring to a boil over medium-high heat. Reduce the heat and simmer for 30 to 45 minutes, or until the leeks are tender. Add the parsley and reserved chicken. Let cool, then refrigerate, covered, for at least 8 hours, or overnight.

4 About 1 hour before serving, make the matzo balls: In a medium bowl, whisk together the schmaltz or oil and eggs. In another small bowl, mix the matzo meal and salt together. Add the matzo meal to the eggs and mix well. Add the seltzer and mix until smooth. Cover and refrigerate for 20 minutes.

5 Bring a large pot of water to a boil over medium-high heat. Reduce the heat, and drop matzo balls approximately 1½ inches in diameter into the barely simmering water. Cover and cook for 20 to 30 minutes, or until the matzo balls are cooked through. With a slotted spoon, transfer the matzo balls to a bowl.

6 To serve, remove the fat layer from the soup and reheat the soup over medium heat until hot. Add the matzo balls and cook for 3 to 5 minutes, or just until heated through.

7 Ladle the soup and matzo balls into large bowls, and garnish with the parsley.

ADVANCE PREPARATION
The soup may be made up to 2 days ahead. The matzo balls can be made up to 4 hours ahead, covered, and left at room temperature.

Butternut Squash and Chestnut Soup with Chipotle Cream

➜ **With its vibrant orange** squash base, sweet undertone of maple syrup, and creamy chestnut flavor, I call this my "Taste of Autumn Soup." A swirl of smoky chipotle cream adds a Southwestern touch. I like to serve small mugs of this during the holidays when company arrives.

Serves 4 to 6

2 tablespoons olive oil
2 leeks, white part only, cleaned and finely chopped
1 pound peeled and seeded butternut squash, diced (or one 1½-pound squash, peeled, seeded, and diced)
One 7- to 8-ounce bottle roasted or steamed chestnuts
2 garlic cloves, minced
4 cups chicken or vegetable broth
2 teaspoons maple syrup
Salt and freshly ground black pepper
2 tablespoons fresh lemon juice
¼ cup Chipotle Cream (page 161)
2 tablespoons finely chopped fresh chives for garnish

1 In a large saucepan, heat the oil over medium-high heat. Add the leeks and sauté for 5 minutes, or until softened. Add the squash and chestnuts and cook, stirring, for 3 minutes or until nicely coated with oil. Add the garlic and cook for 1 minute. Add the broth and syrup and season with salt and pepper, stir well, and bring to a boil. Reduce the heat to medium-low, cover, and simmer for 20 to 25 minutes, or until the chestnuts and squash are very soft. Add the lemon juice.

2 Puree the soup with a hand blender. Or puree in a regular blender in batches, or in a food processor, and return the soup to the pot. Reheat if necessary, and taste for seasoning.

3 To serve, ladle the soup into soup bowls. Swirl a tablespoon of Chipotle Cream into each one, and garnish with the chopped chives.

ADVANCE PREPARATION
The soup may be prepared up to 3 days in advance, covered, and refrigerated. Reheat gently. The soup also freezes well. Adjust the seasonings when you reheat the soup.

MAIN COURSES: *poultry*

Rosemary-Orange Glazed Chicken

Braised Chicken with Caramelized Onions and Wild Mushrooms

Roast Chicken Breasts with Mexican Pesto Sauce

Spicy Chicken Gumbo

Chicken Paillards with Pistachio Pesto Vinaigrette

Chicken Agrodolce

Roasted Hoisin Turkey Breast with Cranberry Fruit Chutney
and Make-ahead Gravy

Turkey Potpie with Puff Pastry Crust

Crispy Roast Duck with Lavender Honey Sauce

Rosemary-Orange Glazed Chicken

→ **This is one of those gems** of a recipe that will become a family favorite. I like the sweet citrus orange flavor tempered by the woodsy fresh rosemary. I also like that the yams make this a complete meal.

Serves 4

MARINADE
Grated zest and juice of 1 orange
4 garlic cloves, minced
2 tablespoons olive oil
1 tablespoon white balsamic vinegar
1 tablespoon finely chopped
  fresh rosemary
Salt and freshly ground black pepper

One 4-pound chicken, cut into serving
  pieces
2 yams (about 1 pound), peeled and
  cut into 1-inch dice
1 leek, white and light green parts only,
  cleaned and finely chopped
Grated zest and juice of 1 orange
1 tablespoon finely chopped fresh rosemary,
  plus rosemary sprigs for garnish

1 *To make the marinade:* In a small bowl, combine ingredients and mix until blended. Taste for seasoning. Place the chicken in a lock-top plastic bag and pour in the marinade, turning to coat the chicken. Make sure the marinade is evenly distributed, seal the bag, and refrigerate for 30 minutes to 4 hours.

2 Preheat the oven to 425°F. Place the chicken, with the marinade, in a large shallow roasting pan. Place the yams and leek around the chicken, stirring to coat them with the marinade.

3 Roast the chicken for 1 hour to 1 hour and 10 minutes, or until it is cooked through with no pinkness remaining and the skin is brown and crispy. Transfer to a serving platter. (You may need to remove the breasts earlier, since they cook faster than the other parts of the chicken. Cover with foil to keep warm.)

4 To finish the sauce, place the roasting pan over medium-high heat. Add the orange zest, juice, and chopped rosemary and reduce the sauce, stirring, for about 2 minutes, until slightly thickened. Taste for seasoning.

5 Pour the sauce over the chicken, spoon the yams and leek around, and garnish with rosemary sprigs. Serve immediately.

ADVANCE PREPARATION
The chicken may be marinated up to 4 hours ahead.

Braised Chicken with Caramelized Onions and Wild Mushrooms

➤ *Reminiscent of coq au vin,* this combines earthy dried mushrooms and crispy smoked bacon, along with sweet caramelized onions, to lend a rich depth of flavor. It's the kind of dinner I yearn for on a chilly evening. I like to serve this right out of the braising pan. Roasted Fennel (page 136) and steamed baby potatoes are good accompaniments.

Serves 4 to 6

1 ounce dried wild mushrooms, such as shiitake or porcini
6 slices applewood-smoked bacon (about 4 ounces), cut into 1-inch pieces
One 4-pound chicken, cut into serving pieces; plus 2 chicken breast halves if serving 6
Salt and freshly ground black pepper
2 onions, very thinly sliced
1 cup full-bodied red wine, such as Merlot, Cabernet Sauvignon, or Zinfandel, or as needed

20 garlic cloves, peeled and root ends trimmed
1 teaspoon tomato paste
¼ teaspoon dried thyme
2 tablespoons balsamic vinegar or 1 tablespoon Balsamic Syrup (page 166)
2 tablespoons finely chopped fresh parsley for garnish

1 Trim the stems of the mushrooms if necessary, and place the mushrooms in a heatproof bowl. Pour boiling water to cover over them and let stand for 30 minutes, or until softened. Lift the mushrooms out of the liquid and strain the liquid into a bowl. Reserve 1¼ cups of the liquid. Finely chop the mushrooms and set aside.

2 In a deep sauté pan large enough to hold the chicken in a single layer, sauté the bacon over medium heat, turning to cook evenly, for about 6 to 8 minutes, until very crisp and brown. Remove with a slotted spoon and drain on paper towels.

3 Season the chicken with salt and pepper. Increase the heat to medium-high and brown the chicken in the bacon fat, in batches if necessary, turning to brown evenly, for about 3 to 4 minutes per side. Transfer to a platter and set aside.

4 Pour off all but 3 tablespoons of the fat from the pan, and add the onions to the pan. Cover and cook, stirring occasionally, for about 8 minutes, or until lightly browned. Add ½ cup of the red wine and stir up the brown bits to deglaze the pan. Cook, uncovered, for about 8 minutes, stirring occasionally, until the onions are caramelized. Add the garlic, strained mushroom liquid, the remaining ½ cup wine, the tomato paste, thyme, and salt and pepper to taste and bring to a boil over high heat, scraping up any brown bits.

5 Reduce the heat to medium and add the reserved mushrooms and the chicken. Turn the chicken to coat it, then turn skin-side up, cover, and cook over low heat, turning the chicken once, for about 25 to 30 minutes, or until no pinkness remains in the meat. If the pan gets dry, add a little more wine.

6 Transfer the chicken to a platter. Add the balsamic vinegar to the pan and boil to reduce it for 1 minute. Add the bacon and taste for seasoning. Return the chicken to the pan for serving, or pour the sauce over the chicken on the platter. Garnish with the parsley and serve immediately.

ADVANCE PREPARATION
The chicken may be made up to 1 day ahead, covered, and refrigerated. Bring to room temperature and then reheat in a 350°F degree oven for 20 minutes, or until heated through.

Roast Chicken Breasts with Mexican Pesto Sauce

➜ *Yum!* This is a variation on one of my all-time favorite recipes from *The Taste of Summer.* Marinated in wine and Mexican Pesto, this dish is as inviting as its original. The chicken is stuffed under the skin with a savory bread crumb pesto filling and roasted until crisp. Accompany it with Butternut Squash and Corn Enchiladas with Salsa Verde and Chipotle Cream (page 122). You can also serve the chicken in bite-sized pieces as an hors d'oeuvre, with toothpicks.

Serves 6 to 8

MARINADE
¼ cup dry white wine
¼ cup Mexican Pesto (page 159)
Salt and freshly ground black pepper

8 large skin-on boneless chicken breast halves (about ⅔ to ¾ pound each)

SAUCE
½ cup Mexican Pesto (page 159)
1 tablespoon red wine vinegar
½ cup crème fraîche
Salt and freshly ground black pepper

STUFFING
1 cup dried bread crumbs or panko (Japanese bread crumbs)
3 tablespoons freshly grated Parmesan cheese
2 tablespoons Mexican Pesto (page 159)
Salt and freshly ground black pepper

Fresh cilantro leaves for garnish

1 *To make the marinade:* In a small bowl, combine all the ingredients and mix well. Taste for seasoning.

2 Place the chicken in a lock-top plastic bag and pour in the marinade, turning to coat the chicken. Make sure the marinade is evenly distributed, seal the bag, and refrigerate for at least 30 minutes.

3 While the chicken marinates, make the sauce: In a small bowl, combine all the ingredients and whisk until smooth. Taste for seasoning, cover, and refrigerate.

4 Preheat the oven to 425°F.

5 *To make the stuffing:* In a medium bowl, combine all the ingredients and mix together until the pesto has been absorbed by the bread crumbs. Remove the chicken breasts from the marinade and place skin-side up in a large roasting pan or on a rimmed baking sheet. Place a heaping tablespoon of stuffing underneath the skin of each breast, carefully lifting up the skin, without tearing it, and spreading the stuffing evenly over the meat. Place the skin back down and pat it to help distribute the stuffing.

6 Roast the chicken for 20 to 25 minutes, or until golden brown and crisp. If the breasts cook through before the skin crisps, remove them from the oven and turn the oven to broil. Broil the chicken for 3 to 5 minutes, until the skin is very crisp. Drain off any excess oil.

7 Arrange the chicken breasts on a serving platter and spoon about 1 tablespoon of sauce on each one. Garnish with cilantro and serve immediately.

ADVANCE PREPARATION

The sauce may be prepared up to 1 day in advance; remove from the refrigerator 30 minutes before serving. The marinade may also be prepared up to 1 day in advance. The chicken can marinate for up to 4 hours.

Spicy Chicken Gumbo

→ **There are many versions** of this Southern staple, but all gumbos have a deep dark roux, okra, and filé powder in common (filé powder is ground sassafras leaves that thicken and add a woodsy flavor). Sautéing the okra gives it a golden brown color and lovely flavor. You'll find Cajun Creole spice in the spice section of your supermarket. Serve the gumbo with steamed rice if you like. To begin a meal, try Grapefruit, Mushroom, and Avocado Salad (page 36). I often serve this on New Year's Day or Super Bowl Sunday.

Serves 6

½ cup, plus 2 tablespoons canola oil
½ pound okra, trimmed and cut into ½-inch-thick slices
2 pounds boneless, skinless chicken thighs, cut into 2-inch pieces
6 tablespoons all-purpose flour
1 large onion, chopped
1 red bell pepper, cored, seeded, and diced
1 green bell pepper, cored, seeded, and diced
3 garlic cloves, minced
5 cups chicken broth

One 14½-ounce can diced tomatoes, with their juice
2 bay leaves
2½ to 3 tablespoons Cajun Creole seasoning blend
Salt and freshly ground black pepper
1 teaspoon filé powder
½ pound andouille sausage, sliced into 1-inch pieces
2 tablespoons finely chopped fresh parsley
Hot pepper sauce

1 In a large Dutch oven, heat 2 tablespoons of the oil over medium heat. Add the okra and sauté, stirring occasionally, for about 12 to 15 minutes, or until golden brown and softened. Transfer to a bowl and set aside.

2 Add another 2 tablespoons of oil to the pot and heat over medium-high heat. Sauté the chicken, in batches, for about 3 to 5 minutes, or until lightly browned. Transfer to a platter and set aside.

3 Add the remaining 6 tablespoons oil to the pot and heat for 2 minutes, or until very hot. Add the flour and whisk until incorporated. Cook this roux for about 4 minutes, or until dark brown, stirring constantly with a wooden spoon. Be careful not to let the roux burn. Add the onion and bell peppers, reduce the heat to medium, and cook for about 8 to 10 minutes, or until the vegetables are softened, stirring occasionally. Add the garlic and cook for another minute.

4 Add the okra, chicken broth, diced tomatoes, bay leaves, and seasoning blend, and season with salt and pepper. Bring to a boil, then lower the heat and simmer gently for about 20 minutes, or until the gumbo is lightly thickened. Add the sautéed chicken and cook for another 10 minutes, or until the chicken is cooked through.

5 Add the filé powder and sausage and cook for 3 minutes, or until the sausage is heated through. Remove the bay leaves and taste for seasoning.

6 Ladle the gumbo into bowls. Garnish with the parsley, and pass the hot sauce.

ADVANCE PREPARATION
The gumbo may be made up to 3 days ahead, covered, and refrigerated. Reheat gently, and adjust the seasoning before serving.

Chicken Paillards with Pistachio Pesto Vinaigrette

Chicken paillards, thin scallops, lend themselves to last-minute preparations with a minimum of fuss. Sautéing them over very high heat so they cook through quickly ensures that they will be very tender. The Pistachio Pesto Vinaigrette makes a very tasty but surprisingly easy sauce. Add a bit of lemon zest to the vinaigrette for extra flavor. Serve this with Penne with Leeks, Broccoli Rabe, and Pistachio Pesto Sauce (page 107).

Serves 4 to 6

VINAIGRETTE
⅓ cup **Basic Vinaigrette** (page 167)
1 tablespoon **Pistachio Pesto** (page 158)

6 large skinless, boneless chicken breast
  halves (about 6 ounces each)

1 **lemon, halved**
¼ cup **Pistachio Pesto** (page 158)
Salt and freshly ground black pepper

1 In a small bowl, combine the vinaigrette and pesto and mix until blended. Set aside.

2 Place each chicken breast half between 2 pieces of plastic wrap and, using a mallet or the bottom of a saucepan, pound to an even ⅛-inch thickness. Place the paillards on a baking sheet and squeeze the lemon juice over both sides. Spread a thin layer of pesto on both sides of each paillard. Season with salt and pepper.

3 Heat a nonstick skillet or grill pan over medium-high heat and spray with olive oil. When the skillet is hot, cook the paillards, in batches, for about 2 to 3 minutes on each side, or until just cooked through.

4 Place the chicken on serving plates and spoon over the vinaigrette. Serve immediately.

Chicken Agrodolce

→ *My friend and fellow cook* Laurie Burrows Grad loves all things Italian. This is an adaptation of her version of *agrodolce*, a sweet and sour sauce, from southern Italy. The sauce also goes well with zucchini and pork, but I like it best with chicken. Chicken thighs work well for braising. Make this a day ahead if you can, to let the flavors marry. Serve with steamed rice, couscous, or lightly buttered hot penne.

Serves 6

¼ cup pine nuts
12 boneless chicken thighs
Salt and white pepper
2 tablespoons olive oil
1 large onion, finely chopped
2 large stalks celery, finely chopped
2 large carrots, peeled and finely chopped
3 tablespoons all-purpose flour
¾ cup dry white wine

¼ cup white wine vinegar or rice wine vinegar
2 tablespoons sugar
2 cups chicken broth
1 bay leaf
½ cup golden raisins
¼ cup capers, drained and rinsed
Fresh mint leaves for garnish

1 Preheat the oven to 350°F. Spread the nuts on a small baking sheet and toast them for about 5 minutes, or until lightly browned and fragrant. Set aside.

2 Heat a nonstick grill pan over medium-high heat, and spray with olive oil. Season the chicken on both sides with salt and pepper. Cook the chicken, in batches, for 5 minutes, or until golden on the first side, then turn and cook for 4 to 5 minutes on the second side, or until golden. Transfer the chicken to a plate and set aside, covered to keep warm.

3 In a large Dutch oven or deep heavy saucepan, heat the olive oil over medium heat. Add the onion, celery, and carrots and sauté for 10 minutes, stirring often, or until just softened. Add the flour and stir for about 1 minute, or until blended and smooth.

4 Increase the heat to high and add the wine, vinegar, and sugar. Boil for a minute or two, stirring until thickened. Add the broth, bay leaf, and chicken and bring to a boil. Reduce the heat to low, partially cover, and simmer slowly for about 15 minutes, stirring occasionally. Turn the chicken and simmer for another 15 minutes, or until the chicken is cooked through. Remove the bay leaf.

5 Add the raisins and capers and stir to combine. Increase the heat and bring to a simmer, then reduce the heat to low and simmer for 5 minutes. Add the pine nuts.

6 Serve the chicken hot, garnished with mint leaves.

ADVANCE PREPARATION
This dish is best prepared a day in advance and refrigerated. The next day, the fat can easily be removed. Reheat gently.

Roasted Hoisin Turkey Breast with Cranberry Fruit Chutney and Make-ahead Gravy

→ *Roasting a boneless turkey breast* solves the problem of stuffing and carving a whole bird. I like this Asian-inspired marinade because it adds a bold flavor without overwhelming the other traditional Thanksgiving dishes. The easy-to-prepare no-fail gravy can be made a few days in advance and then reheated just before serving; I like to add the defatted turkey drippings for extra flavor. For a full-bodied taste, finish it off with a little hoisin sauce.

If I am having a large crowd, I do cook a whole turkey as well as a turkey breast. For the whole turkey, simply double the amount of marinade, rub the marinade all over the turkey and under the skin, and marinate overnight. An unstuffed 16-pound turkey will take about 4 hours or so to roast at 325°F (add another hour for a stuffed turkey); a thermometer inserted in the thickest part of the thigh should register 170°F and the juices should run clear. Cover the bird with foil, after 1 hour, to avoid burning the skin.

Serve this with Rustic Mashed Potatoes with Mascarpone and Chives (page 131) or Corn Bread, Chestnut, and Dried Fruit Dressing (page 137) and Green Beans with Glazed Shallots and Lemon (page 128). For dessert, consider Pumpkin-Chocolate Bread Pudding (page 151) or Persimmon Crostini with Honeyed Mascarpone and Pomegranate Seeds (page 155).

Serves 6 to 8

MARINADE
2 medium shallots, finely chopped
2 garlic cloves, minced
2 tablespoons hoisin sauce
1 tablespoon balsamic vinegar
1 tablespoon soy sauce
Freshly ground black pepper
3 tablespoons olive oil

One 3½-pound boned and tied turkey breast
½ cup chicken broth

GRAVY
½ cup (1 stick) unsalted butter
½ cup all-purpose flour
3½ cups turkey or chicken broth, warmed
½ cup dry red wine
Salt and freshly ground black pepper

2 cups Cranberry Fruit Chutney (page 165)

1 *To make the marinade:* In a small bowl, whisk together all the ingredients.

2 Place the turkey breast in a large lock-top plastic bag and pour in the marinade; turn the turkey to coat evenly. Seal the bag and refrigerate for 3 to 4 hours.

3 Preheat the oven to 350°F. Transfer the turkey to a roasting pan and pour the remaining marinade over it. Cover the pan tightly with foil, and roast for 1¼ hours.

4 Increase the oven temperature to 400°F. Remove the foil and brush the turkey with the marinade in the pan. Pour in the broth and roast for about 15 to 20 more minutes, or until an instant-read thermometer inserted into the thickest part of the breast registers 170°F, basting with the pan juices halfway through the cooking time. The skin should be a deep brown color.

5 Transfer the turkey to a platter and let rest for about 20 minutes before carving. Strain the pan drippings into a gravy separator and set aside.

6 *To make the gravy:* In a large heavy saucepan, melt the butter over medium heat. Slowly whisk in the flour, then whisk briskly until bubbles form. Continue whisking for 3 to 5 minutes, or until the roux thickens and turns a golden brown; the color is important, because it will determine the color of the gravy.

7 Add the warm broth and wine, whisking until completely blended. Cook over medium heat for 15 to 20 minutes, until the gravy is thickened and no taste of flour remains. Pour in the defatted reserved pan drippings, whisking to incorporate completely. Season with salt and pepper.

8 Serve the turkey with the gravy and the chutney.

ADVANCE PREPARATION
The turkey may be made through Step 2 up to 4 hours ahead. The gravy, without the pan drippings, may be made up to 3 days ahead, covered, and refrigerated; reheat gently before continuing.

Turkey Potpie with Puff Pastry Crust

→ *When I was growing up,* we always had a freezer full of store-bought chicken potpies. This recipe bears little resemblance to the pies of my childhood memories. It is brimming with mushrooms, fresh baby carrots, leeks, peas, and corn and topped with a golden brown Parmesan puff pastry crust. This homey dish works well for a weekday dinner or a weekend gathering with friends. I like to start with Autumn Salad with Persimmons and Pomegranates (page 37). For dessert, try Chocolate Fudge Pie (page 145) or Chocolate Peanut Butter Brownies (page 150) with French vanilla ice cream.

Serves 6

1 pint (about 2 cups) pearl onions or one 10-ounce bag frozen pearl onions, defrosted

3 medium carrots, peeled and cut into 1-inch pieces or 10-ounce bag peeled baby carrots

1 pound Yukon Gold potatoes, peeled and cut into 1-inch pieces

1/2 cup (1 stick) unsalted butter

2 leeks, white and light green parts only, cleaned and finely chopped

3/4 pound medium cremini mushrooms, thickly sliced

1 cup frozen petite peas, defrosted

1 cup frozen corn kernels, defrosted

4 cups 2-inch chunks cooked turkey breast (1 1/2 pounds)

7 tablespoons all-purpose flour

2 cups turkey or chicken broth

1 cup half-and-half

Salt and white pepper

3 tablespoons finely chopped fresh parsley

2 tablespoons finely chopped fresh chives

1 sheet frozen puff pastry (half of a Pepperidge Farm box), defrosted

1 large egg, beaten

2 tablespoons freshly grated Parmesan cheese

1 Put the pearl onions in a large bowl. Add the carrots and potatoes to a medium pan of boiling water and simmer for about 10 minutes, or until tender. Drain and add to the onions.

2 In a medium skillet, melt 2 tablespoons of the butter over medium heat. Add the leeks and sauté for about 3 minutes, or until softened. Add the mushrooms and sauté for 3 minutes, or until softened. Add the leeks and mushrooms, along with the cooking juices, to the vegetables in the bowl. Add the peas, corn, and turkey, mix well, and set aside.

3 Preheat the oven to 400°F. In a large saucepan, melt the remaining 6 tablespoons butter over medium heat. Sprinkle in the flour and cook, whisking constantly, for 3 minutes or until the roux is blond colored. Slowly add the broth and half-and-half, whisking constantly, and whisk for about 3 more minutes, until the sauce is thickened and smooth. Season with salt and pepper. Pour the sauce over the turkey mixture, add the herbs, and mix well. Taste for seasoning.

4 Butter a large 2-inch-deep casserole dish (about 9 by 13 inches). Pour the turkey mixture into the casserole.

CONTINUED

5 If necessary, roll out the pastry on a lightly floured surface to a 14-by-10-inch rectangle. Brush the rim of the casserole dish with water. Cover the filling with the pastry, pressing it against the rim of the dish. Make 3 slashes in the pastry. Brush the crust with the beaten egg.

6 Place the dish on a baking sheet and bake for 40 to 45 minutes, or until the filling is bubbling. Sprinkle with the Parmesan cheese during the last 15 minutes of baking to brown the crust. Let the potpie sit for 10 minutes before serving.

ADVANCE PREPARATION

The potpie may be assembled 1 day ahead, covered well, and refrigerated. Remove the pie from the refrigerator before preheating the oven. It may also be baked ahead and refrigerated, covered. Bring to room temperature and then reheat in a 325°F oven for 20 minutes, or until the filling is bubbling.

Crispy Roast Duck with Lavender Honey Sauce

→ The biggest challenge in cooking duck is the abundance of fat underneath the skin. A good solution is to cook it at 275°F, which allows the fat to render and keeps the meat moist and tender. This two-step process enables you to cook the ducks ahead and still serve a crisp bird. I like Muscovy ducks because they have a high proportion of breast meat; look for them fresh at specialty supermarkets.

The lavender honey glaze and sauce are a welcome change from the classic orange sauce. Accompany this with Autumn Noodles and Rice (page 111) and Braised Spinach with Leeks and Roasted Garlic (page 129). Quartering the ducks is the easiest way to serve them.

Serves 4 to 6

GLAZE
3 tablespoons lavender honey
2 tablespoons boiling water
1 teaspoon coarsely ground black pepper

Two 4$\frac{1}{2}$-pound ducks, neck and giblets
    removed
Salt and freshly ground black pepper
2 cups boiling water

SAUCE
2 tablespoons unsalted butter
3 medium shallots, minced
1 cup demi-glace
1 tablespoon plus 1 teaspoon
    lavender honey
2 teaspoons red wine vinegar
Salt and freshly ground black pepper

1 *To make the glaze:* In a small bowl, combine the honey, boiling water, and pepper, stirring to blend. Set aside.

2 Preheat the oven to 275°F. Season the ducks with salt and pepper. With a kitchen fork, prick the skin about $\frac{1}{4}$ inch deep all over, particularly in the fatty area around the thighs and the wing area; do not pierce the meat. Place the ducks breast-side down on a rack in a roasting pan. Pour the boiling water over them. Roast for 2 hours.

3 Turn the ducks breast-side up and brush with the glaze. Roast for another 1 to 1$\frac{1}{4}$ hours, or until the legs wiggle easily. Transfer to a carving board and let cool.

4 Using heavy poultry shears, quarter the ducks; cut the backbones out to make this easier. Place the duck quarters in plastic bags and refrigerate.

5 About 45 minutes before serving, preheat the oven to 375°F. Place the duck skin-side up on a rimmed baking sheet and roast for 30 minutes, or until the duck is cooked through and crisp.

6 Meanwhile, make the sauce: In a small skillet, melt 1 tablespoon of the butter over medium-high heat. Add the shallots and sauté for 2 minutes, or until softened. Add the demi-glace, honey, and vinegar, increase the heat to high, and reduce the sauce to a light glaze, about 3 minutes.

7 Whisk the remaining 1 tablespoon butter into the sauce to thicken it and add a sheen. Season with salt and pepper.

8 Place the duck on a platter and spoon over a little sauce. Serve the remaining sauce on the side.

ADVANCE PREPARATION
The ducks may be prepared through Step 4 up to 8 hours ahead. The sauce can be made through Step 6 up to 4 hours ahead, covered, and kept at room temperature. Add the final tablespoon of butter and the seasoning just before serving.

MAIN COURSES:
meat

Turkey Meat Loaf with Sun-Dried Tomato Pesto Glaze

Sauerbraten

Short Ribs with Dried Mushrooms and Fire-Roasted Tomatoes

Grilled Rib-eye Steaks with Chipotle Sauce

Braised Lamb Shanks with Toasted Almond Gremolata

Medallions of Pork with Apple, Prune, and Apricot Sauce

Pork Chops with Sweet Cherry Peppers

Veal Chops with Grand Café Tapenade

Veal Ragù on Pappardelle

Turkey Meat Loaf with Sun-Dried Tomato Pesto Glaze

→ *Ground turkey and beef* blend well to avoid the denseness I often find in meat loaf. Buttermilk, whole-grain mustard, and Parmesan cheese perk up the flavors, while a sun-dried tomato glaze brings it all together. Serve this hot with Rustic Mashed Potatoes with Mascarpone and Chives (page 131) and roasted whole carrots. Consider Citrus Pudding Cake (page 154) for dessert. The meat loaf is also great cold, sliced and served with assorted condiments, salads, and bread for a tailgate picnic.

Serves 6 to 8

2 slices white bread, crusts removed and torn into 2-inch pieces
1 cup buttermilk
1 carrot, peeled and shredded
4 garlic cloves, minced
2 large eggs
1/2 cup freshly grated Parmesan cheese
1 tablespoon whole-grain mustard
1 teaspoon salt, or to taste

Freshly ground black pepper
1 pound ground beef
1 pound ground turkey

GLAZE
1/2 cup Sun-Dried Tomato Pesto (page 159)
1 teaspoon whole-grain Dijon mustard
2 teaspoons Balsamic Syrup (page 166)
1/4 cup freshly grated Parmesan cheese

1 Preheat the oven to 350°F. Lightly oil a 9-by-5-by-3-inch loaf pan.

2 Place the bread and buttermilk in a large mixing bowl and mix to combine, mashing up the bread to a mush-like consistency. Add the carrot, garlic, eggs, Parmesan, mustard, salt, and pepper and mix with your hands to combine, making sure that the bread is well blended and that there are no large pieces remaining. Add the meat and blend the mixture together evenly, mixing just enough to combine; if you overmix it, the meat loaf will be dense and dry. To test for seasoning, heat a small nonstick pan over medium-high heat. Brown a small piece of the meat mixture on all sides, then cook through and taste for seasoning. Add salt and pepper to the meat loaf mixture if necessary.

3 Pat the meat mixture gently into the prepared loaf pan; don't press it down too firmly.

4 *To make the glaze:* In a small bowl, combine the pesto, mustard, Balsamic Syrup, and 2 tablespoons of the Parmesan cheese. Spoon the glaze over the top of the meat loaf, spreading it evenly over the loaf. Sprinkle the remaining 2 tablespoons cheese evenly over the top.

5 Bake the meat loaf for about 1 1/4 hours, or until it has begun to shrink away from the sides of the pan and an instant-read thermometer registers 145°F. Let stand for 15 minutes. Drain the fat from the loaf. Serve hot or cold.

ADVANCE PREPARATION
This may be made up to 2 hours ahead and set aside at room temperature. Reheat in a 350°F oven for 20 minutes, or until hot. It may be also made up to 2 days ahead, covered, and refrigerated, to be served cold.

Sauerbraten

I tasted sauerbraten for the first time when I was in college. The memory of that meal lingered, and over the years I tried to replicate the dish, with more surprises than I could have imagined. Many failed attempts only strengthened my determination. Finally, talks with colleagues and butchers led me to change the cut of meat and lower the cooking temperature. Those changes resulted in the following recipe, which replicates that memorable meal. You'll need to start this three days ahead, since the meat marinates for two days before cooking. I like to serve this with Braised Red Cabbage in Red Wine (page 125) and Crispy Scallion-Potato Pancakes (page 132).

Serves 8

MARINADE
2 onions, chopped
2 carrots, peeled and chopped
2 stalks celery, chopped
2$\frac{1}{2}$ cups dry red wine
1$\frac{1}{2}$ cups red wine vinegar
1 cup water
12 cloves
1 tablespoon mustard seeds
2 bay leaves
2 tablespoons sugar
2 tablespoons coarse salt
1 tablespoon lightly crushed
    black peppercorns

One 4$\frac{1}{2}$-pound boned, rolled,
    and tied top round roast
3 tablespoons olive oil
2 carrots, peeled and chopped
1 onion, chopped
10 gingersnaps, finely crushed
Salt and freshly ground black pepper

1 *To make the marinade:* In a medium saucepan, combine all the ingredients and bring to a boil over high heat. Boil for 2 minutes. Remove from the heat and let cool.

2 Place the roast in a large lock-top plastic bag and pour in the marinade. Seal the bag and put it in another bag to prevent leakage. Refrigerate, turning every 12 hours, for 2 days.

3 Preheat the oven to 300°F. Remove the meat from the marinade, and reserve the marinade. Blot the beef with paper towels. In a large Dutch oven, heat the oil over medium-high heat. Brown the beef on all sides, about 5 to 8 minutes. Using long tongs, transfer the beef to a plate. Add the carrots and onion to the pot and sauté for about 5 minutes, or until softened.

4 Return the meat to the pot. Strain the marinade over the meat and bring to a boil over high heat. Cover the pot, place in the oven, and braise for about 3$\frac{1}{2}$ to 4 hours, until the meat is tender; turn the meat halfway through the cooking process. Test by sticking a fork into the meat: it should come out easily.

5 Transfer the meat to a cutting board and let stand for 10 minutes; set the pot aside. Slice the meat and place in a deep heatproof serving dish.

6 To finish the sauce, add the gingersnaps to the pot and boil over medium-high heat for about 3 minutes, or until slightly thickened. Season with salt and pepper if necessary. Pour the sauce over the meat and serve immediately.

ADVANCE PREPARATION
This may be made up to 2 days ahead, covered, and refrigerated. Reheat in a 350°F oven for 30 to 45 minutes, or until the sauce is bubbling.

Short Ribs with Dried Mushrooms and Fire-Roasted Tomatoes

→ *These short ribs* take time to prepare, so plan accordingly. Make them at least a day ahead of time to allow the flavors to come together. Freeze any leftovers, and you'll have a comforting entrée all ready to reheat on a moment's notice. Serve with Rustic Mashed Potatoes with Mascarpone and Chives (page 131).

Serves 6

6 pounds lean beef short ribs, patted dry
Salt and freshly ground black pepper
1½ ounces dried mushrooms, such as shiitake or porcini
3 cups beef broth or water
2 tablespoons olive oil
¼ pound thickly sliced pancetta, cut into ½-inch dice
3 medium yellow onions, coarsely chopped
4 medium carrots, peeled and thinly sliced
One 14½-ounce can fire-roasted crushed tomatoes
1 cup chicken or beef broth
½ cup prune juice

3 tablespoons balsamic vinegar
6 garlic cloves, sliced in half
2 sprigs fresh thyme or ½ teaspoon dried thyme
2 tablespoons finely chopped fresh parsley

FOR FINISHING THE SAUCE
1½ cups chicken or beef broth
1 tablespoon prune juice
1 teaspoon balsamic vinegar
Salt and freshly ground black pepper

2 tablespoons finely chopped fresh parsley for garnish

1 Preheat the oven to 450°F. Place the ribs in a large roasting pan and salt and pepper them evenly on both sides. Roast for 25 minutes. Turn them over and roast for another 25 minutes, or until the ribs are very brown. Transfer to a platter, blot with paper towels, and set aside. Turn the oven temperature down to 325°F.

2 Meanwhile, trim the stems of the mushrooms if necessary. In a small saucepan, combine the mushrooms and beef broth, bring to a boil over high heat, and boil for 5 minutes. Or place the broth and mushrooms in a glass measuring cup and microwave on high for 4 minutes. Cover and let stand for 10 minutes. Lift the mushrooms out of the liquid and strain the liquid into a bowl. Chop the mushrooms and add to the liquid. Set aside.

3 In a large nonstick Dutch oven or heavy flameproof casserole, heat the oil over medium-high heat. Add the pancetta and sauté for about 4 minutes, until brown and crispy. Transfer to a bowl and set aside.

4 Add the onions to the pot and sauté, stirring often so they don't burn, for about 10 to 12 minutes, or until brown and slightly caramelized. Add the carrots and sauté for 3 more minutes, or until slightly softened. Add the mushrooms and their broth, the pancetta, tomatoes, chicken broth, prune juice, vinegar, garlic, and herbs to the pot and bring to a boil.

5 Place the short ribs in the pot and spoon over some of the vegetables. Place in the oven and bake for about 2½ hours, or until the meat is tender. Transfer the beef to a platter and let cool. Let the sauce cool in the pot.

6 Place the short ribs in a covered container or a lock-top plastic bag and refrigerate. Refrigerate the sauce directly in the pot. (It is best to do this for at least 8 hours, or, preferably, overnight.)

7 Remove the layer of fat from the sauce, and remove any accumulated fat on the ribs. Gently reheat the sauce over medium heat. When it is hot, add the 1½ cups broth, the prune juice, and vinegar, and season with salt and pepper and bring to a boil. Add the ribs and heat through, about 10 minutes. Taste for seasoning.

8 Place the beef and sauce in a large serving bowl and garnish with the parsley. Serve immediately.

ADVANCE PREPARATION
This may be made up to 3 days ahead, covered, and refrigerated. It may also be frozen. Defrost before reheating. Gently reheat on top of the stove, and adjust the seasonings before serving.

Grilled Rib-eye Steaks with Chipotle Sauce

→ *Chipotle puree infuses* a traditional wine sauce with a smoky flavor, and a swirl of crème fraîche adds extra body. This version of the traditional steak au poivre is great for entertaining because the sauce can be made ahead of time. Serve with Potato and Onion Gratin (page 130) and Braised Spinach with Leeks and Roasted Garlic (page129). For dessert, try Chocolate Fudge Pie (page 145).

Serves 6 to 8

SAUCE
2 tablespoons unsalted butter
4 medium shallots, minced
1 cup dry red wine
1 cup veal or beef stock
1 to 1½ teaspoons Chipotle-Garlic
   Puree (page 160)

2 to 3 tablespoons crème fraîche, to taste
Salt and freshly ground black pepper

Four 1-pound rib-eye steaks,
   about ¾ inch thick
Salt and freshly ground black pepper
Watercress or parsley sprigs for garnish

1 *To make the sauce:* In a medium heavy saucepan, melt the butter over medium heat. Add the shallots and sauté for about 3 to 5 minutes, until soft. Add the red wine, increase the heat to high, and boil for about 5 minutes, until reduced by half to a syrupy glaze. Add the stock and chile puree and reduce for about 5 to 8 minutes, until the sauce barely coats the back of a spoon. Add the crème fraîche and reduce for another few minutes, until the sauce coats the spoon again. Season with salt and pepper, and set aside.

2 Prepare a grill or a grill pan for medium-high-heat grilling. Season the steaks lightly with salt and pepper. Grill the steaks for 4 to 5 minutes on each side, or until medium-rare. Or place in the grill pan and cook, turning once until medium-rare. Transfer the steaks to a carving board and let rest for 10 minutes.

3 While the steaks are resting, gently reheat the sauce.

4 Cut the steaks into ½-inch-thick slices. Spoon some sauce onto each serving plate and arrange the steak slices, slightly overlapping, on top. Garnish with watercress and serve immediately.

ADVANCE PREPARATION
The sauce may be prepared up to 4 hours ahead, covered, and refrigerated. Reheat gently.

Braised Lamb Shanks with Toasted Almond Gremolata

➙ *The flavors and aromas* of this dish remind me of a long-ago stay in Paris, when my husband and I would wander around Place Saint-Michel searching for the most delicious platters of couscous. Our favorite haunt served lamb surrounded by a large mound of couscous, vegetables, and potatoes. A bowl of spicy harissa sauce was available to heat up the dish. I've added my own twist with a toasted almond gremolata for another layer of flavor. Try this for a dinner party, served with Couscous with Leeks, Currants, and Mint (page 115).

Serves 6 to 8

6 lamb shanks (about 1 1/4 pounds each)
Salt and freshly ground black pepper
1/4 cup olive oil
2 onions, finely chopped
3 carrots, peeled and finely chopped
4 garlic cloves, minced
1 teaspoon ground cumin
1/2 teaspoon ground cinnamon
1/2 teaspoon ground coriander
1/4 teaspoon ground ginger
1/4 teaspoon ground nutmeg
1/4 teaspoon ground allspice
1/4 teaspoon crushed red pepper flakes, or to taste

1 1/2 cups chicken broth
1 cup dry red wine, such as Merlot or Zinfandel
One 28-ounce can fire-roasted diced tomatoes, drained
2 tablespoons tomato paste

GREMOLATA
1/3 cup sliced or chopped almonds
3 tablespoons finely chopped fresh cilantro
3 tablespoons finely chopped fresh mint
2 garlic cloves, minced
1 teaspoon grated orange zest

1 Preheat the oven to 325°F. Season the lamb shanks evenly with salt and pepper.

2 In a Dutch oven or other very large heavy flameproof casserole, heat 2 tablespoons of the oil over medium-high heat. Brown the lamb shanks, in two batches, for about 8 to 10 minutes, or until nicely browned on all sides. Transfer to a bowl and set aside.

3 Pour off all the drippings and add the remaining 2 tablespoons oil to the pot. Reduce the heat to medium, add the onions and carrots, and sauté for 4 to 6 minutes, until lightly browned and softened. Add the garlic and all the spices and sauté for another minute, or until very fragrant, stirring constantly.

4 Add the broth, wine, diced tomatoes, and tomato paste and bring to a boil over medium-high heat. Season with salt and pepper. Arrange the browned lamb shanks in the pot, making sure that they are all halfway covered with the liquid. Cover and braise in the oven for about 3 hours, turning them every hour, until the meat is extremely tender.

5 While the lamb is cooking, make the gremolata: Toast the almonds in a nonstick skillet over medium-high heat, tossing or stirring them constantly, for about 3 minutes, until lightly browned. Transfer to a small bowl and let cool.

CONTINUED

6 Add the remaining ingredients to the almonds and mix well. Set aside.

7 When the shanks are cooked, transfer them to a serving platter and cover with foil. Strain the pan juices into a bowl, reserving the vegetables, and skim the fat from the juices. Return the vegetables and juices to the pot and reduce over high heat for about 10 minutes, until slightly thickened. Taste the sauce for seasoning.

8 Return the shanks to the pot and heat until very hot. Place the shanks, with the sauce, on the platter, and sprinkle the gremolata evenly on top. Serve immediately.

ADVANCE PREPARATION

The lamb shanks may be prepared up to 2 days ahead, covered, and refrigerated. Reheat gently. It is best to make the gremolata the same day so the herbs will be fresh.

Medallions of Pork with Apple, Prune, and Apricot Sauce

Pork tenderloins are easy to prepare and very versatile. Grill them whole with a dry rub, or cut them into medallions and quickly sauté them, as in this dish. Dried apricots and prunes, along with fruity Gewürztraminer wine, sweetly flavor the pork. Serve with Roasted Jerusalem Artichokes and Carrots (page 127).

Serves 6 to 8

SAUCE
½ cup diced dried apricots
½ cup diced pitted prunes
1 cup Gewürztraminer
3 tablespoons unsalted butter
3 shallots, finely chopped
1 medium pippin or other firm tart apple, peeled, cored, and cut into 1-inch pieces
⅓ cup heavy (whipping) cream
¾ cup beef or chicken broth
Salt and freshly ground black pepper

1 tablespoon unsalted butter
2 tablespoons olive oil
2 large pork tenderloins (about 1¼ pounds each), each cut into 6 medallions about 2 inches thick
Salt and freshly ground black pepper
½ cup Gewürztraminer
½ cup chicken broth
2 tablespoons heavy (whipping) cream
2 tablespoons finely chopped fresh parsley for garnish

1 *To make the sauce:* In a small saucepan, combine the dried fruit and Gewürztraminer and bring to a boil over high heat. Remove from the heat and let macerate for 10 minutes.

2 Meanwhile, in a large skillet, melt the butter over medium-high heat. Add the shallots and sauté for about 2 to 3 minutes, or until softened and browned. Add the apples and sauté for 2 to 3 minutes, or until nicely coated with butter. Add the macerated fruit, with the wine, the cream, and broth and simmer for 5 more minutes, or until slightly thickened and the alcohol has burned off. Season with salt and pepper. Set aside.

3 In another large skillet, melt the butter with the oil over medium-high heat. Season the medallions with salt and pepper, add to the pan, and cook for about 5 minutes, until browned on the first side. Turn over with tongs and cook for about another 4 minutes, until browned on the second side and just cooked through. Transfer the medallions to a platter and cover with foil.

4 Pour off the drippings. Add the Gewürztraminer to the pan and deglaze, scraping up the brown bits. Add the sauce, broth, and cream and bring to a simmer. Simmer, stirring, for 2 minutes, or until slightly thickened.

5 Spoon the sauce over the pork, garnish with the parsley, and serve immediately.

Pork Chops with Sweet Cherry Peppers

➜ *My friend* and occasional cooking partner Kathy Blue loves pork chops. She enjoyed this unique dish at the Globe restaurant in Venice, California, and passed on her version to me. So quick, so easy, yet so tasty, these pork chops are simmered with bottled sweet cherry peppers to punch up their flavor. Adding a few chopped-up hot cherry peppers is recommended for those who can take the heat. Accompany with simple buttered noodles.

Serves 4

Four $\frac{1}{2}$-pound center-cut pork chops, about 1 $\frac{1}{2}$ inches thick
Salt and freshly ground black pepper
3 tablespoons olive oil
1 medium red onion, cut into eighths

One 16-ounce jar sweet cherry peppers, drained, $\frac{1}{2}$ cup juice reserved
4 garlic cloves, minced
1 sprig thyme
1 cup chicken broth

1 Preheat the oven to 425°F. Season the pork chops on both sides with salt and pepper.

2 In a 12-inch heavy skillet or flameproof casserole, heat the oil over medium-high heat. Add the pork chops and cook for about 3 minutes on each side, or until nicely browned. Transfer to a plate.

3 Add the onion and drained cherry peppers to the pan and sauté, stirring occasionally, for about 4 to 5 minutes, until the onion is translucent. Add the garlic and thyme and sauté for another minute. Add the chicken broth and reserved $\frac{1}{2}$ cup pepper juice and bring to a boil over high heat.

4 Return the pork chops to the pan, along with any juices. Place in the oven and roast for about 15 minutes, or until the pork chops are cooked through. Transfer the pork chops to a platter.

5 Place the pan back on the stove over high heat and reduce the sauce for about 3 to 5 minutes, or until slightly thickened. Spoon the sauce around the pork chops and serve immediately.

Veal Chops with Grand Café Tapenade

→ *San Francisco's Grand Café* makes a mean tapenade: a fresh herb combination of thyme, tarragon, and basil infuses the sun-dried tomato–olive mixture. I like to sear the veal chops on the grill, then lightly spread them with tapenade and finish them off in the oven. You can use the remaining tapenade in a marinade or salad dressing, or spread it on toasted French bread as an appetizer. Serve these with Pasta Salad with Roasted Vegetables (page 108) or Potato and Onion Gratin (page 130).

Serves 4

TAPENADE

3 garlic cloves, peeled
½ cup oil-packed sun-dried tomatoes
¼ cup pitted Kalamata olives
1 tablespoon capers
1 teaspoon anchovy paste or 1 anchovy fillet
½ cup fresh basil leaves
1 tablespoon fresh tarragon leaves
1 teaspoon fresh thyme leaves
¼ cup olive oil
Freshly ground black pepper

MARINADE

3 tablespoons olive oil
2 tablespoons balsamic vinegar
1 shallot, finely chopped
1 teaspoon Tapenade (from above)
Salt and freshly ground black pepper

Four ¾-pound veal rib chops
Salt and freshly ground black pepper
Thyme sprigs for garnish

1 *To make the tapenade:* In a food processor, mince the garlic. Add the remaining ingredients except for the oil and pepper and pulse until finely minced but with some texture remaining. Add the oil and pulse once or twice to combine. Season with pepper and pulse to mix. Transfer to a small container and set aside.

2 *To make the marinade:* In a small bowl, combine the ingredients. Taste for seasoning. Brush both sides of the veal chops with the marinade and place in a lock-top plastic bag. Seal the bag. Refrigerate for at least 2 hours.

3 Preheat the oven to 450°F. Prepare a grill for medium-heat grilling or heat a grill pan over high heat. Spray the grill pan with nonstick cooking spray.

4 Remove the veal chops from the marinade and season with salt and pepper. Place on the grill or in the grill pan and cook for 5 minutes. Turn over and smear a teaspoon of tapenade on each chop. Cook for about 4 more minutes, until rare.

5 Transfer the veal to a baking sheet and finish cooking in the oven, about 5 more minutes, or until the veal is very pink inside.

6 To serve, place the veal chops on serving plates and garnish with thyme sprigs.

ADVANCE PREPARATION
The veal may be marinated up to 4 hours ahead. The tapenade can be covered and refrigerated for up to 2 weeks.

Veal Ragù on Pappardelle

→ *A taste of Italy,* this dish is hearty and comforting. The veal cooks down into a rich tomato-wine sauce. Pappardelle, thick ribbons of pasta, is perfect with the sauce. Bring a wedge of Parmigiano-Reggiano or Pecorino Romano to the table with a grater and serve each guest a fresh sprinkling of cheese. The sauce freezes well, so you might want to make a double batch and save some for a rainy day. Begin with Sliced Fennel Salad with Lemon Parmesan Dressing (page 41).

Serves 4 to 6

RAGÙ
¼ cup olive oil
2 carrots, peeled and finely chopped
1 large onion, finely chopped
2 stalks celery, finely chopped
1 red bell pepper, cored, seeded, and finely chopped
4 garlic cloves, minced
Salt and freshly ground black pepper
¼ pound thickly sliced pancetta, cut into ½-inch pieces

2 pounds boneless veal shoulder, cut into ½-inch dice
1 cup dry red wine
One 28-ounce can diced tomatoes, with their juice
1 cup chicken broth
1 sprig rosemary
½ teaspoon crushed red pepper flakes
1 teaspoon Balsamic Syrup (page 166)

1 pound pappardelle
A wedge of Parmesan or Pecorino Romano cheese

1 *To make the Ragù:* In a large Dutch oven, heat 2 tablespoons of the olive oil over medium heat. Add the carrots, onion, celery, and bell pepper and sauté for about 10 to 12 minutes, until softened. Add the garlic and sauté for another minute. Season with salt and pepper. Transfer to a bowl and reserve.

2 Add the remaining 2 tablespoons oil to the pot and increase the heat to medium-high. Add the pancetta and brown, stirring, for about 3 minutes. Add the veal, in batches, and cook, stirring, for about 10 minutes, until evenly browned. Return all the veal to the pot.

3 Add the wine and deglaze the pot by scraping up the browned bits. Add the reserved cooked vegetables, the tomatoes, broth, rosemary, and red pepper flakes. Season with salt and pepper. Bring to a boil, then reduce the heat to low and simmer, stirring occasionally, for about 1¼ hours, or until the meat is very tender. Add the Balsamic Syrup and taste for seasoning.

4 Meanwhile, cook the pappardelle according to the package directions. Drain, reserving about ½ cup of the pasta liquid, and place the pasta in a large deep skillet.

5 Add half of the meat sauce and some of the reserved pasta liquid to the pappardelle, toss with tongs to coat evenly, and cook for another minute. Transfer to a serving bowl and spoon on the remaining sauce. Serve, grating some cheese on top of each serving.

ADVANCE PREPARATION
The sauce may be made up to 3 days ahead, covered, and refrigerated. The sauce may also be frozen for up to 2 months. Reheat gently, and adjust the seasoning before serving.

MAIN COURSES:
seafood

Seafood Stew with Garlic Toasts and Lemon Parmesan Aïoli

Scallops with Herbed Tomato-Wine Sauce

Shrimp Nasi Goreng

Grilled Halibut with Asian Plum Sauce

Roasted Tilapia with Salsa Verde Glaze

Whole Roasted Striped Bass with Roasted Vegetables

Roasted Salmon with Pistachio Pesto Crust

Citrus Swordfish on Warm Spicy Slaw

Seafood Stew with Garlic Toasts and Lemon Parmesan Aïoli

This quick stew is great on a cold, blustery day. The aromas remind me of sipping soup in a seaside Mediterranean village. The base of the stew can be made ahead and then finished at the last minute, making this an excellent choice for entertaining. For a variation, substitute your favorite fish, such as halibut or sea bass. Begin with Frisée Salad with Bacon and Goat Cheese (page 39). For dessert, try Maple Walnut Tart (page 146).

Serves 4 to 6

2 tablespoons olive oil
1 onion, finely chopped
1 carrot, peeled and finely chopped
1 fennel bulb, trimmed, cored, and
   finely chopped
4 garlic cloves, minced
1½ cups dry red wine
1 cup bottled clam juice, or as needed
½ cup water
One 28-ounce can diced tomatoes,
   with their juice
½ teaspoon anchovy paste
A 2-inch-long strip of orange peel
Salt and freshly ground black pepper

TOASTS
1 garlic clove, sliced in half
12 slices French bread
Olive oil spray

AÏOLI
¼ cup mayonnaise
2 garlic cloves, minced
1 teaspoon grated lemon zest
1 teaspoon anchovy paste
2 tablespoons freshly grated
   Parmesan cheese
White pepper

12 large shrimp, peeled, with tails left on,
   and deveined
12 medium scallops
2 tablespoons finely chopped fresh chives
   for garnish

1 In a medium soup pot, heat the olive oil over medium-high heat. Add the onion, carrot, and fennel and sauté, stirring occasionally, for about 5 minutes, or until softened. Add the garlic and sauté for another minute. Add the wine, clam juice, water, tomatoes, anchovy paste, orange peel, and salt and pepper and simmer, partially covered, over medium-low heat for 20 minutes.

2 Meanwhile, make the toasts: Preheat the oven to 350°F. Rub the garlic on one side of each slice of bread and very lightly spray with olive oil spray. Place the bread on a baking sheet and toast for 7 to 10 minutes, or until lightly browned. Remove and set aside.

3 *To make the aïoli:* In a small bowl, combine all the ingredients and mix to blend. Taste for seasoning. Set aside.

4 When the soup base is cooked, remove the orange zest, and season to taste. With a hand blender, blend until it is roughly pureed, with some texture remaining. Or transfer to a regular blender, in batches, and roughly puree, then return to the pot. If the soup base is too thick, add a bit more water or clam juice.

CONTINUED

Seafood Stew with Garlic Toasts
and Lemon Parmesan Aïoli CONTINUED

5 Set the pot over medium-high heat, and bring to a simmer. Add the shrimp and scallops and simmer for about 3 to 4 minutes, or until just cooked through.

6 To serve, spread some aïoli on each toast. Ladle the stew into soup bowls (I like to use shallow soup plates for a pretty presentation). Arrange 2 or 3 toasts around the edge of each bowl and dollop a teaspoon of aïoli in the center. Garnish with the chopped chives, and serve immediately.

ADVANCE PREPARATION

The stew may be made through Step 4 up to 2 days ahead, covered, and refrigerated. Reheat before continuing. Make the toasts the day you will serve the stew.

Scallops with Herbed Tomato-Wine Sauce

→ **This dish really delivers** on the promise of minimum cooking time with maximum flavor. I like using the larger sea scallops; if you prefer bay scallops, make sure to sauté them quickly so they don't get overcooked. For a casually elegant presentation, serve these in large shallow ramekins. Accompany this with Autumn Noodles and Rice (page 111) or Roasted Jerusalem Artichokes and Carrots (page 127).

Serves 4 to 6

SAUCE
2 tablespoons olive oil
2 leeks, white and light green parts only, cleaned and finely chopped
¾ pound cremini mushrooms, sliced
6 garlic cloves, minced
1 cup canned crushed tomatoes
½ cup dry white wine
2 tablespoons finely chopped fresh parsley
Salt and freshly ground black pepper
2 teaspoons balsamic vinegar

¼ cup all-purpose flour
Salt and freshly ground black pepper
1½ pounds sea scallops
3 tablespoons olive oil
¼ cup dry white wine
2 tablespoons finely chopped fresh parsley for garnish

1 *To make the sauce:* In a large skillet, heat the olive oil over medium-high heat. Add the leeks and sauté for 3 minutes, or until softened. Add the mushrooms and sauté for another 3 to 4 minutes, or until softened. Add the garlic and sauté for 1 minute, or until softened but not browned. Add the tomatoes, wine, parsley, and salt and pepper and bring to a simmer. Reduce the heat to medium and cook for about 3 to 5 minutes, or until the sauce is slightly thickened. Add the vinegar and cook for another minute. Taste for seasoning, and set aside.

2 Place the flour in a lock-top plastic bag, season with salt and pepper, and shake to mix. Place the scallops in the bag, seal it, and shake the bag until the scallops are lightly coated with the flour.

3 In a large skillet, heat the olive oil over medium-high heat. Add the scallops and cook for about 2 minutes on each side, or until golden brown. Add the wine and deglaze the pan by scraping up the brown bits. Add the tomato sauce to the scallops, bring to a simmer, and stir to coat the scallops.

4 Transfer the scallops and sauce to a serving dish and garnish with the parsley. Serve immediately.

Shrimp Nasi Goreng (Indonesian-Style Fried Rice)

→ *I enjoyed this unusual rice dish* at a friend's house and have been making it ever since. Spicy and full of bright flavors, this Indonesian fried rice is just the thing to make when you are looking for a new taste.

For the best result, the rice should be allowed to cool to room temperature before making the dish. If the rice is warm, it will become oily when stir-fried. The cooking goes quickly, so be sure to have all ingredients prepared and ready. I like to use serrano chiles, but any small flavorful hot chile will work well. Peanuts may not be authentic, but they taste delicious! Begin with Grapefruit, Mushroom, and Avocado Salad (page 36) and finish with Citrus Pudding Cake (page 154) for dessert.

Serves 6

NOTE
When working with chiles, always wear rubber gloves. Wash the cutting surface and knife right afterward.

3 cups water
1½ cups long-grain white rice
¼ cup peanut oil
3 carrots, peeled and diced
½ pound mushrooms, diced
1 red bell pepper, cored, seeded, and diced
1 pound large shrimp, peeled, deveined, and cut into 1-inch pieces
3 scallions, white and light green parts only, finely chopped
3 shallots, thinly sliced
3 garlic cloves, minced

1 tablespoon minced fresh ginger
2 small green or red chiles, seeded and finely chopped (see Note)
1 teaspoon paprika
2 tablespoons ketchup
2 tablespoons soy sauce
Salt and freshly ground black pepper
¼ pound fresh bean sprouts (about 2 cups)

¼ cup peeled, seeded, and diced cucumber for garnish
½ cup roasted peanuts for garnish

1 At least 3 hours ahead, cook the rice: In a large saucepan with a lid, bring the water to a boil over medium-high heat. Add the rice, turn the heat down to medium-low, cover, and simmer gently for about 20 minutes, or until the rice is tender and the water is absorbed. Transfer the rice to a large cookie sheet or sheet of wax paper, separating any clumps of rice, and let cool.

2 Just before serving, in a large wok, heat 2 tablespoons of the oil over high heat. When the oil is almost smoking, add the carrots, mushrooms, and bell pepper and stir-fry for about 1 minute, or until slightly softened. Add the shrimp and scallions and cook, tossing every 15 to 20 seconds, for 1 to 2 minutes, or until the shrimp just turn pink. Transfer the vegetables and shrimp to a bowl and set aside.

3 Add the remaining 2 tablespoons oil to the wok. When the oil is almost smoking, add the shallots and stir-fry for about 1 to 2 minutes, or until lightly browned. Add the garlic, ginger, and chiles and toss for about 30 seconds, or until they are aromatic.

4 Add the rice and spread it over the bottom and halfway up the sides of the wok. Let cook for about 10 seconds, then toss to combine and coat the rice. Add the paprika, ketchup, and soy sauce and toss to mix. Add the reserved vegetables and shrimp and toss again to distribute the ingredients evenly. Season with salt and pepper. Add the bean sprouts and toss once more. Taste for seasoning.

5 Transfer to a large serving bowl or platter and garnish with the cucumber and peanuts. Serve immediately.

ADVANCE PREPARATION
The rice may be cooked up to 8 hours (and no less than 3 hours) before stir-frying. Cover loosely and keep at room temperature.

Grilled Halibut with Asian Plum Sauce

→ **When you're in a hurry** but want great taste, try this Asian-style fish dish. The slightly sweet plum sauce complements the halibut's mild flavor. For a satisfying weeknight dinner, accompany the fish with Green Beans with Glazed Shallots and Lemon (page 128) and steamed rice.

Serves 4 to 6

SAUCE
1 teaspoon dry mustard
2 tablespoons rice or cider vinegar
2 teaspoons soy sauce
1 teaspoon Asian sesame oil
$\frac{1}{4}$ cup Chinese-style plum sauce
2 tablespoons hot water

2 tablespoons finely sliced scallions
Salt and freshly ground black pepper

Four $\frac{1}{2}$-pound halibut fillets or steaks, about 1 $\frac{1}{2}$ inches thick
2 tablespoons finely sliced scallions for garnish

1 *To make the sauce:* In a bowl, combine all of the ingredients and mix until completely blended and smooth. Taste for seasoning.

2 Place the halibut in a lock-top plastic bag and pour ¼ cup of the sauce over it. Turn the fish in the bag to coat evenly. Close the bag and marinate the fish for at least 30 minutes in the refrigerator.

3 Prepare a barbecue for medium-high-heat grilling or heat a grill pan over high heat. Spray the grill pan with nonstick cooking spray. Remove the fillets from the marinade and place on the grill or in the grill pan. Cook for about 5 minutes per side, or until cooked through and opaque.

4 Place the fillets on serving plates and spoon over some of the remaining sauce. Garnish with the scallions and serve immediately.

ADVANCE PREPARATION
The fish may be marinated up to 2 hours ahead.

Roasted Tilapia with Salsa Verde Glaze

→ *I like to use this spicy glaze* on delicate fillets like tilapia because of their smooth texture and mild flavor; farm-raised tilapia are becoming readily available in supermarkets. Salsa combined with mayonnaise becomes a golden brown glaze when cooked at high heat. You can substitute store-bought fresh salsa verde if you are in a hurry. Serve this with Autumn Noodles and Rice (page 111).

Serves 4

GLAZE
Juice of $\frac{1}{2}$ lime
$\frac{1}{4}$ cup mayonnaise (low-fat may be used)
$\frac{1}{2}$ teaspoon Chipotle-Garlic Puree (page 160)
$\frac{1}{4}$ cup Salsa Verde (page 162)
Salt and freshly ground black pepper

Four $\frac{1}{3}$- to $\frac{1}{2}$-pound tilapia fillets
2 tablespoons chopped fresh cilantro
  for garnish

1 Preheat the oven to 425°F.

2 *To make the glaze:* In a small bowl, combine the ingredients and mix well. Taste for seasoning.

3 Place the fillets on a baking sheet and spread the glaze evenly on top of each one. Roast for 10 to 12 minutes, or until the fish is cooked through and opaque and the topping is golden brown; be careful not to let the glaze burn.

4 Using a large spatula, carefully transfer the fish to serving plates. Garnish with the cilantro and serve immediately.

ADVANCE PREPARATION
The glaze may be prepared up to 1 day ahead, covered, and refrigerated.

Whole Roasted Striped Bass
with Roasted Vegetables

Looking for an impressive presentation for a special occasion? Here it is. The roasted vegetables are spooned into the center of a large platter and the whole roasted fish are placed on top. And although this looks complicated, it is relatively easy to put together.

Asian markets are a good source of very fresh fish. Select fish based on the signs of freshness: clear eyes, moist-looking and firm flesh, and no indication of strong odors (fish should smell like the ocean). For dessert, consider the comforting Butterscotch Pudding (page 153) or Maple Walnut Tart (page 146).

Serves 4 to 6

2 striped bass (2½ pounds each), cleaned
  and scaled, head and tail left on
¼ cup olive oil
2 tablespoons fresh lemon juice
2 garlic cloves, minced
1 teaspoon salt
Freshly ground black pepper
1 lemon, thinly sliced
6 sprigs thyme
2 sprigs rosemary
Reserved fennel fronds (see following)

VEGETABLES
2½ pounds small fingerling or baby Dutch
  potatoes, well scrubbed

1 fennel bulb, trimmed, cored, and
  finely chopped
20 garlic cloves, root ends trimmed
2 sprigs thyme
1 sprig rosemary
2 tablespoons olive oil
Salt and freshly ground black pepper
2 pounds cherry or grape tomatoes, halved

2 tablespoons unsalted butter, softened
Juice of 1 lemon
1 tablespoon sherry vinegar
3 tablespoons finely chopped fresh parsley
  for garnish

1 Rinse the fish thoroughly inside and out under cold running water to remove any blood. Cut 3 diagonal slashes on both sides of each fish. Set the fish in a large shallow baking dish, letting the heads and tails hang over the sides a little if necessary.

2 Combine the olive oil, lemon juice, garlic, and salt in a small bowl. Rub the mixture into the sides and cavity of each fish. Sprinkle pepper into the cavities and stuff with the lemon slices, thyme and rosemary sprigs, and reserved fennel fronds. Cover and refrigerate to marinate for 20 to 30 minutes.

3 Meanwhile, preheat the oven to 450°F.

4 *To make the vegetables:* Lightly coat a large roasting pan or rimmed baking sheet with nonstick cooking spray. Place the potatoes, fennel, garlic, thyme, and rosemary in the pan. Drizzle with the olive oil and toss to coat well. Sprinkle with salt and pepper, toss again, and spread out in an even layer. Roast the vegetables for about 15 minutes, stirring every 5 minutes, until they begin to get brown and crispy.

CONTINUED

Whole Roasted Striped Bass
with Roasted Vegetables CONTINUED

5 Remove the pan from the oven. With a spatula, move the vegetables to the side. Gently lift the fish from the marinade and place them on an angle, side by side. Rub half of the butter over the top of each fish. Place the pan in center of oven and roast for 10 minutes per inch of thickness at the thickest part of the fish, about 25 minutes. During the last 10 minutes of cooking, add the tomatoes to the vegetables, stirring to combine, and continue roasting until the tomatoes are soft and the fish is just cooked through and opaque.

6 Carefully transfer the fish to a platter, and transfer the vegetables to a serving platter large enough to accommodate the fish. Use a metal spatula to scrape the crisp brown vegetable pieces in the bottom of the pan onto the platter. Cover with foil to keep warm.

7 Bone the fish: Starting at the neck of one fish, slit the skin along the back down to the tail. Cut down to the bone behind the head. Open out the fish and gently lift the backbone off the flesh; remove any remaining belly bones. Fold the top fillet back over so that the fish is whole once again. Repeat with the second fish. Place the fish diagonally on top of the vegetables and sprinkle with the lemon juice, vinegar, and parsley.

8 To serve, cut the fish into individual pieces and serve with the vegetables.

Roasted Salmon with Pistachio Pesto Crust

Four ½-pound salmon fillets, each about
  1 inch thick
1 tablespoon fresh lemon juice
Salt and freshly ground black pepper

6 tablespoons dried bread crumbs
  or panko (Japanese bread crumbs)
2 tablespoons Pistachio Pesto (page 158)

→ *Roasting the salmon* in a very hot oven nicely browns and crisps the pistachio pesto crust. Make sure not to overcook the fish; I like salmon best prepared medium-rare. Serve with Penne with Leeks, Broccoli Rabe, and Pistachio Pesto Sauce (page 107).

Serves 4

1 Preheat the oven to 450°F. Place the fish in an oiled roasting pan and sprinkle on the lemon juice. Season with salt and pepper.

2 In a small bowl, combine the bread crumbs and pesto, mixing well. Pat the mixture on top of the fish in an even layer.

3 Roast the fish for 10 to 15 minutes, or until it's brown and crispy. Serve immediately.

ADVANCE PREPARATION
This may be made through Step 1 up to 2 hours ahead, covered, and refrigerated.

Citrus Swordfish on Warm Spicy Slaw

→ *Swordfish can be fixed* in so many ways, and it always tastes different. It's good in chowder, or grilled as brochettes; here it's a meal in itself. A twist on coleslaw, the warm spicy slaw pairs nicely with the grilled citrus swordfish. Begin with Grapefruit, Mushroom, and Avocado Salad (page 36). For dessert, serve Apple, Pear, and Dried Cherry Almond Crisp (page 140).

Serves 4

MARINADE
Grated zest of 1 lime
1 tablespoon fresh lime juice
2 tablespoons rice vinegar
2 garlic cloves, minced
1 tablespoon finely chopped ginger
3 tablespoons olive oil
1 tablespoon soy sauce
Freshly ground black pepper to taste

Four 1/3- to 1/2-pound swordfish steaks, no more than 3/4 inch thick

SLAW
2 tablespoons pine nuts
3 tablespoons peanut oil
1 leek, white and light green parts only, cleaned and finely chopped
2 carrots, peeled and cut into matchsticks
1/2 red bell pepper, cored, seeded, and cut into matchsticks
1 medium green cabbage, cored and finely shredded
1 teaspoon Asian chili paste with garlic
1/4 cup dry sherry
2 tablespoons soy sauce
Salt and freshly ground black pepper

1 *To make the marinade:* In a medium bowl, combine the ingredients and whisk until blended.

2 Place the fish in a lock-top plastic bag and pour the marinade over it. Turn the fish in the bag to coat evenly. Close the bag and marinate the fish for at least 30 minutes in the refrigerator.

3 Shortly before serving, make the slaw: In a large deep skillet, toast the pine nuts over medium heat for about 3 to 5 minutes, shaking the pan constantly to avoid burning the nuts. Transfer to a plate and set aside.

4 Add the oil to the same skillet and heat over medium-high heat. Add the leek and sauté for about 3 minutes, or until slightly softened. Add the carrots and bell pepper and sauté for about 3 more minutes, or until crisp-tender, stirring occasionally. Add the cabbage and sauté for 3 minutes longer, or until just wilted.

5 Add the chili paste, sherry, soy sauce, and salt and pepper and stir to combine. Bring to a boil and cook for 1 minute. Taste for seasoning and add the pine nuts. Set aside, covered to keep warm, while you grill the fish.

6 Prepare a barbecue for medium-high-heat grilling, or heat a grill pan over high heat. Spray the pan with nonstick cooking spray. Remove the fish from the marinade and place on the grill or in the pan. Cook for 3 to 5 minutes on each side, depending on the thickness and until desired doneness.

7 To serve, spoon some slaw onto each serving plate. Cut each swordfish steak in two and arrange the pieces at an angle to each other on top of the slaw.

ADVANCE PREPARATION
The fish may be marinated up to 2 hours ahead.

PASTA, GRAINS, *and* LEGUMES

Fusilli with Pink Vodka Sauce and Velvet Chicken

Penne with Leeks, Broccoli Rabe, and Pistachio Pesto Sauce

Pasta Salad with Roasted Vegetables

Autumn Noodles and Rice

Polenta Lasagna Bolognese

Couscous with Leeks, Currants, and Mint

Winter Squash and Red Swiss Chard Risotto

White Bean and Arugula Stew Gratinée

Fusilli with Pink Vodka Sauce and Velvet Chicken

→ *I often make this* when I am in a hurry. Poaching the chicken and letting it cool in the liquid ensures a velvet-like texture. Cream gives the tomato sauce its distinctive pink color. While there are many similar ready-made sauces on the grocery shelf, this "from-scratch" version is almost as quick but more flavorful. Begin your meal with Grapefruit, Mushroom, and Avocado Salad (page 36).

Serves 4 to 6 as
a main course

SAUCE
4 cups chicken broth or water,
  or as needed
Salt
1 pound skinned and boned chicken
  breasts
1 tablespoon olive oil
1 leek, white and light green parts only,
  cleaned and finely chopped
4 cups homemade marinara sauce
  or favorite store-bought sauce

¼ cup sun-dried tomato pesto, homemade
  (page 159) or store-bought
¼ cup vodka
½ cup heavy (whipping) cream
  or crème fraîche
Pinch of crushed red pepper flakes

1 pound fusilli or penne
Freshly grated Parmesan cheese
  for serving

1 *To make the sauce:* In a deep medium skillet or a medium saucepan, bring enough chicken broth and/or water to cover the chicken to a simmer. If using only water, add ½ teaspoon salt. Add the chicken breasts and simmer for 10 to 12 minutes, or until just tender. Remove the pan from the heat and let the chicken cool in the liquid.

2 Drain the chicken and cut or shred into ½-inch-thick slices. Set aside.

3 In a large deep skillet or saucepan large enough to hold the pasta, heat the olive oil over medium heat. Add the leek and sauté, stirring occasionally, for about 5 minutes, until soft but not brown. Add the marinara sauce, pesto, vodka, cream, red pepper flakes, and salt to taste. Bring to a simmer and cook for 3 to 5 minutes to make sure the alcohol has burned off.

4 Add the chicken to the sauce and heat briefly. Taste for seasoning.

5 Meanwhile, cook the pasta according to the package directions. Drain, reserving ½ cup of the pasta water.

6 Add the pasta to the sauce, then add enough of the reserved pasta water to the sauce to give it a nice consistency, and toss well. Serve immediately, passing the Parmesan cheese separately.

ADVANCE PREPARATION
The sauce may be prepared through Step 3 up to 4 hours ahead, covered, and refrigerated; refrigerate the chicken separately. Reheat the sauce gently before adding the chicken.

Penne with Leeks, Broccoli Rabe, and Pistachio Pesto Sauce

→ **The bitterness** of the broccoli rabe offsets the sweet golden leeks and the herbal pistachio pesto in this vegetarian pasta dish. Serve on its own as a main course, or serve it alongside Chicken Paillards with Pistachio Pesto Vinaigrette (page 63). For a nonvegetarian version, it is also nice with some grilled shrimp thrown in at the last minute.

Serves 4 to 6 as
a main course

2 tablespoons olive oil
3 medium leeks, white and light green
   parts only, cleaned and finely chopped
1 pound broccoli rabe, trimmed
   and chopped
1½ cups vegetable broth

¼ cup Pistachio Pesto (page 158)
Salt
Pinch of crushed red pepper flakes
1 pound penne
Freshly grated Pecorino Romano
   for serving

1 In a large deep skillet or saucepan large enough to hold the cooked pasta, heat the oil over medium heat. Add the leeks and sauté for 5 to 6 minutes, or until soft and golden brown. Add the broccoli rabe and sauté, tossing with tongs, for 2 more minutes, or until slightly softened. Add the broth, cover, and cook for 4 to 5 minutes, or until the broccoli rabe is tender. Add the pesto, salt, and red pepper flakes and cook for another minute, until well blended.

2 Meanwhile, cook the penne according to the package directions. Drain, reserving ½ cup of the pasta liquid.

3 Add the pasta to the sauce and toss to coat. Add some of the pasta water if it is too dry. Taste for seasoning. Serve immediately, and pass the grated cheese on the side.

ADVANCE PREPARATION
The sauce may be prepared up to 2 hours ahead, covered, and left at room temperature. Reheat before serving.

Pasta Salad with Roasted Vegetables

→ *This is great for family gatherings,* equally appropriate at a picnic or a simple buffet. Feel free to improvise by adding cooked chicken or seafood. Serve alongside Roasted Salmon with Pistachio Pesto Crust (page 101) or cold sliced Turkey Meat Loaf with Sun-Dried Tomato Pesto Glaze (page 72).

Serves 8 as a side dish

6 scallions, white and light green parts, thinly sliced

4 medium zucchini, sliced

3 bell peppers, red and/or yellow, cored, seeded, and cut lengthwise into strips

2 cups cherry tomatoes

Salt and freshly ground black pepper

¼ cup olive oil

2 cups fresh (about 4 ears) or defrosted frozen corn kernels

1 pound fusilli, bow ties, or penne

DRESSING

3 tablespoons whole-grain mustard

2 medium garlic cloves, minced

¼ cup fresh lemon juice

2 tablespoons sherry vinegar

Salt and freshly ground black pepper

½ cup extra virgin olive oil

¼ cup finely chopped fresh parsley

¼ cup finely chopped fresh basil

½ cup freshly grated Parmesan cheese

1 Preheat the oven to 425°F. Place the scallions, zucchini, bell peppers, and cherry tomatoes in a roasting pan. Season with salt and pepper and toss with the olive oil to coat evenly. Roast for 20 minutes, turning the vegetables once during cooking.

2 Add the corn to the pan and roast for 15 to 20 more minutes, or until the vegetables are very tender and lightly browned. Let cool.

3 Cook the pasta according to the package directions. Drain well.

4 Place the pasta in a large bowl, add the vegetables, and mix well.

5 *To make the dressing:* In a small bowl, combine the mustard, garlic, lemon juice, sherry vinegar, and salt and pepper. Slowly whisk in the olive oil until blended. Pour over the pasta and vegetables, then sprinkle on the chopped herbs and Parmesan and mix to combine evenly. Taste for seasoning. Refrigerate until chilled before serving.

ADVANCE PREPARATION

This may be prepared up to 1 day ahead.

Autumn Noodles and Rice

→ *Red and yellow bell peppers* are at their peak in the autumn months. Fine egg noodles and rice are mixed together in this unusual dish, and toasted almonds add a nice crunch. Serve alongside Braised Chicken with Caramelized Onions and Wild Mushrooms (page 56) or Medallions of Pork with Apple, Prune, and Apricot Sauce (page 81).

Serves 6 as a side dish

¼ cup slivered almonds
3 tablespoons olive oil
1¼ cups long-grain white rice
1¼ cups fine egg noodles
3 cups chicken or vegetable broth
Salt and freshly ground black pepper

1 tablespoon unsalted butter
1 medium leek, white and pale green parts only, cleaned and finely chopped
1 medium yellow or red bell pepper, cored, seeded, and cut into ½-inch dice
2 tablespoons finely chopped fresh parsley

1 Preheat the oven to 350°F. Spread the almonds in a pie pan and toast in the oven for 5 minutes, or until lightly browned. Set aside.

2 In a large saucepan, heat 2 tablespoons of the oil over medium heat. Add the rice and egg noodles and cook, stirring, for about 3 minutes, or until evenly coated and very lightly browned. Add the broth and season with salt and pepper, increase the heat to medium-high, and bring to a boil. Stir well with a fork. Reduce the heat to low, cover, and simmer for 15 to 18 minutes, or until the rice is tender and the liquid has been absorbed.

3 Meanwhile, in a medium skillet, heat the butter and the remaining 1 tablespoon oil over medium heat. Add the leek and sauté, stirring occasionally, for about 3 minutes, or until soft. Add the bell pepper and sauté for about 3 to 4 minutes, or until crisp-tender. Remove from the heat.

4 When the rice and noodles are cooked, add the vegetables, almonds, and parsley and toss with a fork. Taste for seasoning, and serve immediately.

ADVANCE PREPARATION
This may be prepared up to 2 hours ahead and kept, covered, at room temperature. Reheat in the top of a double boiler over medium heat for about 10 minutes.

Polenta Lasagna Bolognese

This casserole is the perfect one-dish meal for a crowd. While it takes some time to prepare, you can assemble it well in advance and have it ready to bake just before your guests arrive; it can also be baked ahead, frozen, and then reheated. You will also have some extra meat sauce to freeze and use over pasta for another meal. Make sure to use a deep lasagna pan so it will all fit in.

I like to serve this during the holidays for a family or a casual dinner party. Start with Sliced Fennel Salad with Lemon Parmesan Dressing (page 41) or Marinated Roasted Beets with Orange-Balsamic Vinaigrette (page 40). For dessert, try Mocha Truffle Tart (page 148).

Serves 10 to 12 as a main course

POLENTA
1 tablespoon olive oil
1 small onion, very finely chopped
1 garlic clove, minced
7 cups chicken or vegetable broth
Salt
2 cups instant polenta
3 tablespoons freshly grated Parmesan cheese

MEAT SAUCE
1/4 cup olive oil
1 pound ground sirloin
1 pound ground veal
1/2 cup milk
2 medium onions, finely chopped
2 medium carrots, peeled and finely chopped

4 large garlic cloves, minced
2 cups dry red wine
8 cups favorite tomato sauce (or two 28- to 32-ounce jars marinara sauce)
1 teaspoon dried basil
A 3-inch-long piece Parmesan cheese rind
Salt and freshly ground black pepper

BÉCHAMEL SAUCE
6 tablespoons unsalted butter
6 tablespoons all-purpose flour
3 cups milk, warmed
Pinch of ground nutmeg
Salt and white pepper

1 cup freshly grated Parmesan cheese
2 tablespoons chopped fresh parsley for garnish

1 *To make the polenta:* Lightly spray a deep 11-by-15-inch lasagna dish with olive oil spray and set aside. In a large deep saucepan, heat the oil over medium-high heat. Add the onion and sauté for 5 minutes, or until softened. Add the garlic and sauté for 1 minute, or until softened, being sure not to brown it. Add the broth and salt to taste and bring to a rolling boil. In a thin stream, very slowly add the polenta, stirring constantly with a wooden spoon. Lower the heat and cook for about 3 minutes, stirring constantly to be sure it doesn't stick, until the polenta is very smooth and stiff. Stir in the Parmesan cheese and then quickly pour the polenta into the prepared baking dish; smooth the top with a spatula if necessary. Allow the polenta to sit at room temperature for 2 hours, or until set.

2 *To make the meat sauce:* In a large Dutch oven, heat 2 tablespoons of the olive oil over medium heat. Add the sirloin and veal and cook, stirring and breaking up the meat, for about 4 to 5 minutes, or until lightly browned. Drain off excess fat, using a colander, and return the meat to the pot. Add the milk and simmer for about 3 to 4 minutes, or until the meat has absorbed the milk. Transfer to a bowl, cover, and set aside.

3 Add the remaining 2 tablespoons oil to the pot and heat over medium heat. Add the onions and carrots and sauté, stirring occasionally, for 4 to 6 minutes, or until softened but not browned. Add the garlic and sauté for 1 minute. Add the wine and boil for 3 to 4 minutes, or until it is reduced by one-third. Add the browned meat, the tomato sauce, basil, and cheese rind, and season with salt and pepper, partially cover, and reduce the heat to

CONTINUED

medium-low. Simmer gently, stirring occasionally, for about 35 to 40 minutes, or until the sauce has a deep rich flavor and is nicely thickened. Remove from the heat and remove the cheese rind.

4 Meanwhile, make the béchamel sauce: In a medium saucepan, melt the butter over medium heat. Whisk in the flour and cook, whisking, for about 2 minutes; do not allow the flour to color. Add the warm milk and nutmeg and season with salt and pepper, whisking to blend. Cook the sauce for about 5 minutes longer, or until it coats a spoon. Set aside.

5 Preheat the oven to 375°F. Remove the polenta from the baking dish by inverting it onto a work surface; set the dish aside. Cut the polenta crosswise in half, to make 2 squares (this will make it easier to transfer the polenta back into the baking dish later on). The easiest way to slice the polenta into layers is to use a piece of dental floss: Hold a 2-foot-long piece of floss taut between your hands, place the floss against the side of one of the squares farthest from you, and pull the floss toward you through the center of the square, slicing the polenta into two layers. (Alternatively, you can use a serrated knife to slice the polenta.) Repeat with the second square.

6 Lightly spray the lasagna dish with olive oil spray again. Spread 2 cups of the meat sauce evenly over the bottom of the lasagna dish. Place 2 of the polenta squares side by side on top of the sauce. Spoon over another 2 cups of the meat sauce and then pour 1 cup of the béchamel sauce evenly over it. Smooth with a spatula. Sprinkle with ½ cup of the Parmesan cheese. Place the remaining layer of polenta on top, then 2½ cups more of the meat sauce and the remaining béchamel (reserve the remaining meat sauce for another use). Sprinkle with the remaining ½ cup Parmesan cheese. (The lasagna will be slightly above the edge of the dish.)

7 Place the lasagna dish on a baking sheet to catch any drips. Bake, uncovered, for 35 to 40 minutes, or until the cheese is melted and the lasagna is bubbling. Remove from the oven and let sit for 10 minutes.

8 Garnish the lasagna with the parsley. To serve, cut into portions and use a spoon or spatula to scoop them out onto individual dishes.

ADVANCE PREPARATION

The sauces and polenta may be made up to 1 day ahead, covered, and refrigerated. Reheat the béchamel sauce gently before assembling. The lasagna can also be assembled up to 1 day ahead, covered, and refrigerated. Remove from the refrigerator 1 hour before baking. The baked lasagna may be completely cooled, covered well, and frozen. Defrost and then reheat in a 350°F oven for about 30 minutes before serving

Couscous with Leeks, Currants, and Mint

➔ *Perfect for entertaining* or a weeknight dinner, this takes just a short time to
prepare. Try it with grilled lamb chops or
Braised Chicken with Caramelized Onions
and Wild Mushrooms (page 56). With its
Middle Eastern influences, it also goes well
with Braised Lamb Shanks with Toasted
Almond Gremolata (page 79).

Serves 6 as a side dish

2 tablespoons unsalted butter
2 leeks, white and light green parts only,
  cleaned and finely chopped
3 cups water
1½ cups quick-cooking couscous

¼ cup dried currants
2 tablespoons finely chopped fresh parsley
1 tablespoon finely chopped fresh mint
Salt and freshly ground black pepper

1 In a medium saucepan, melt the butter over medium heat. Add the leeks and sauté
for 5 to 7 minutes, or until nicely softened and lightly browned. Add the water and bring
to a boil. Add the couscous and currants, cover, and remove from the heat. Let stand for
5 minutes.

2 Add the parsley and mint to the couscous, season with salt and pepper, and fluff with
a fork to combine. Taste for seasoning.

3 Spoon into a serving dish and serve immediately.

ADVANCE PREPARATION
*This may be prepared up to 2 hours in advance and kept, covered, at room temperature. Reheat
in the top part of a double boiler over medium heat for about 10 minutes.*

Winter Squash and Red Swiss Chard Risotto

→ *This colorful risotto* is chock-full of winter's freshest and most colorful produce. The sweet orange butternut squash balances the slightly bitter red chard. Make sure to thinly slice both the stalks and the leaves of the Swiss chard for even cooking. Arborio rice, which will produce a creamy consistency, is the key to a great risotto. Serve this as a vegetarian main course or as a side dish for Veal Chops with Grand Café Tapenade (page 84).

Serves 6 as a main course

¼ cup olive oil
3 leeks, white and light green parts only, cleaned and finely chopped
One 2-pound butternut squash, peeled, seeded, and cut into ½-inch dice
1 cup water
1 small bunch red Swiss chard (about ½ pound), trimmed, leaves finely shredded, and stalks thinly sliced
Salt and freshly ground black pepper

5 cups chicken or vegetable broth
½ cup dry white wine
1½ cups Arborio rice
2 tablespoons finely chopped fresh parsley, plus whole leaves for garnish
2 tablespoons finely chopped fresh sage, plus whole leaves for garnish
½ cup freshly grated Parmesan cheese, plus extra for serving

1 In a large deep skillet, heat 2 tablespoons of the olive oil over medium heat. Add the leeks and sauté for about 4 minutes, until softened and lightly browned. Add the squash and sauté for 3 to 5 minutes, or until it is lightly browned. Add the water, cover, and cook for another 5 to 7 minutes, or until the squash is crisp-tender.

2 Add the chard and stir to combine. Cover and cook for 3 more minutes, or until the chard is wilted, stirring once or twice. Remove the lid, increase the heat, and boil for about 1 minute to evaporate excess liquid. Season with salt and the pepper, and set aside.

3 In a medium saucepan, bring the broth and wine to a simmer over medium-high heat. (Or place in a large glass measuring cup and microwave for 2 minutes.)

4 In a heavy large saucepan, heat the remaining 2 tablespoons olive oil over medium heat. Add the rice and stir with a wooden spoon for about 2 minutes, until all the grains are well coated. Pour in ½ cup of the hot broth and stir until all of the stock is absorbed. Continue adding the broth ½ cup at a time, making sure that the rice has absorbed the previous broth addition each time and stirring constantly to prevent burning or sticking. (It will take about 3 to 5 minutes of stirring between each addition.) The rice should become very creamy as you continue to add the broth.

5 Add the vegetable mixture with the last ½ cup of broth, reduce the heat to low, and cook for another 2 minutes. (You may need to use a fork to mix the vegetables with the rice.) Turn off the heat, add the chopped parsley, chopped sage, and ½ cup grated Parmesan, and stir well to combine evenly with the rice.

6 Spoon the risotto into serving bowls and garnish with sage and parsley leaves. Pass additional Parmesan separately.

ADVANCE PREPARATION
This may be made through Step 2 up to 4 hours ahead. Cover and leave at room temperature.

White Bean and Arugula Stew Gratinée

→ A good dish for vegetarians, this simple white bean stew is flavored with tomatoes, balsamic vinegar, and arugula leaves. Pecorino Romano, one of Italy's oldest cheeses, is made from sheep's milk and has a sharper flavor than Parmesan. Here I combine the Pecorino with crisp-textured panko bread crumbs to form a crisp topping. Serve this as an accompaniment to a simple grilled chicken or as a main course.

Serves 6 as a main course, 8 to 10 as a side dish

2 cups dried white beans, such as Great Northern

2 tablespoons olive oil

6 scallions, white and light green parts only, thinly sliced

1 carrot, peeled and chopped

2 garlic cloves, minced

6 fresh sage leaves, chopped

1/4 cup balsamic vinegar

1 cup canned diced tomatoes, drained

5 cups chicken or vegetable broth

1 bunch arugula (about 1/2 pound), stems removed and leaves torn into bite-sized pieces

Salt and freshly ground black pepper

TOPPING

1/4 cup freshly grated Pecorino Romano cheese

1/4 cup panko (Japanese bread crumbs) or dried bread crumbs

1 tablespoon finely chopped fresh parsley

Freshly grated Pecorino Romano cheese for serving

1 In a large bowl, cover the beans with cold water and soak overnight; drain. Or, if you prefer to do a quick-soak method, in a large saucepan, combine the beans and water to cover, bring to a boil, and cook for 2 minutes. Remove from the heat, cover, and let stand for 1 hour; drain.

2 In a medium Dutch oven, heat the olive oil over medium heat. Add the scallions and sauté for about 3 to 5 minutes, or until softened. Add the carrot and sauté for another 3 minutes. Add the garlic and sage and sauté for 1 minute. Add 3 tablespoons of the balsamic vinegar, the tomatoes, broth, and beans and bring to a boil over high heat. Reduce the heat to low, cover, and simmer for about 1 1/4 hours, or until the beans are very tender and falling apart.

3 Mash some of the beans with the back of a spoon to create a creamy consistency. Cook, uncovered, for 5 to 10 minutes, until slightly thickened.

4 Add the arugula, cover, and cook for 3 minutes, stirring once, or until slightly wilted. Add the remaining 1 tablespoon balsamic vinegar, season with salt and pepper, and mix to combine. Taste for seasoning.

5 Meanwhile, preheat the broiler. In a small bowl, place the cheese, bread crumbs, and parsley and mix to combine.

6 Spoon the beans into a gratin dish. Sprinkle the topping evenly over the beans. Place under the broiler for 3 to 4 minutes, or until the bread crumbs and cheese are nicely browned. Watch carefully to prevent burning. Serve immediately, passing the freshly grated Pecorino Romano separately.

ADVANCE PREPARATION

This may be prepared through Step 4 up to 1 day ahead, covered, and refrigerated. Bring to room temperature, then place in a gratin dish and reheat in a 350°F oven for 30 minutes, or until bubbling, before adding the topping and broiling.

Butternut Squash and Corn Enchiladas with Salsa Verde and Chipotle Cream

Braised Red Cabbage with Red Wine

Roasted Jerusalem Artichokes and Carrots

Green Beans with Glazed Shallots and Lemon

Braised Spinach with Leeks and Roasted Garlic

VEGETABLES *and* POTATOES

Potato and Onion Gratin

Rustic Mashed Potatoes with Mascarpone and Chives

Crispy Scallion-Potato Pancakes

Yam Towers with Chipotle Chive Cream

Roasted Fennel

Corn Bread, Chestnut, and Dried Fruit Dressing

Butternut Squash and Corn Enchiladas with Salsa Verde and Chipotle Cream

My close friend Denny Luria gave me the idea for this spectacular combination: corn tortillas stuffed with a puree of winter squash, roasted garlic, and corn. Every time I serve this, my guests beg me for the recipe. You might serve this as a vegetarian main course, along with a simple salad with toasted pumpkin seeds, or as a side dish on a buffet with Roast Chicken Breasts with Mexican Pesto Sauce (page 58). For dessert, try Toasted Coconut Cake (page 143).

Serves 6

ENCHILADAS

One 2-pound butternut squash, peeled, seeded, and cut into 1-inch dice
2 tablespoons olive oil
6 scallions, white and light green parts only, thinly sliced
1 tablespoon Roasted Garlic Puree (page 163)
1 cup fresh (about 2 ears) or defrosted frozen corn kernels
2 tablespoons finely chopped fresh cilantro
Salt and freshly ground black pepper
1 1/2 cups shredded Monterey Jack cheese
1 1/2 cups shredded mozzarella cheese
Twelve 6-inch corn tortillas

1 recipe Salsa Verde (page 162)
1/2 cup Chipotle Cream (page 161)
2 tablespoons finely chopped fresh cilantro for garnish

1 *To make the enchiladas:* Fill the bottom of a large steamer with water and bring to a boil. Using tongs, carefully place the squash on the steamer rack. Cover and steam over medium heat for 15 to 20 minutes, or until fork-tender. Or place the squash in a glass bowl, cover loosely with plastic, and microwave on high for 5 minutes, or until fork-tender. Set aside.

2 In a large skillet, heat the oil over medium-high heat. Add the scallions and sauté for 3 to 4 minutes, or until very soft and lightly browned. Add the cooked squash and garlic puree and cook for 2 to 3 more minutes, mashing the squash with a potato masher. Add the corn and cook for another minute, or until tender. Add the cilantro and salt and pepper and mix to combine. Taste for seasoning. Remove from the heat.

3 Preheat the oven to 350°F. Grease a 9-by-13-inch baking pan.

4 Combine the cheeses in a bowl, mixing them well so they are evenly blended. With tongs, hold each tortilla over the flame of a burner for about 10 seconds to soften it, and place on a plate. Or soften the tortillas briefly in a nonstick skillet.

5 Place a tortilla on a work surface and spread a big tablespoon of the squash filling down the middle of it. Sprinkle 2 tablespoons of the cheese on top, roll up, and place seam-side down in the baking pan. Repeat with the remaining tortillas.

CONTINUED

6 Pour the Salsa Verde evenly over the enchiladas. Sprinkle the remaining cheese over the top. Bake for about 20 to 25 minutes, or until the enchiladas are bubbling and the cheese has melted.

7 To serve, place 2 enchiladas on each plate and put a dollop of the Chipotle Cream on top. Garnish with the cilantro and serve immediately.

ADVANCE PREPARATION

This may be prepared through Step 4 up to 8 hours ahead, covered well, and refrigerated. Bring to room temperature before continuing.

Braised Red Cabbage with Red Wine

→ *Goose fat is the secret ingredient* in
this time-tested classic. You can find frozen
goose fat at European delis, but if necessary, you can use chicken fat or olive oil.
Serve this savory and comforting winter
dish as an accompaniment to Sauerbraten
(page 73), with Crispy Scallion-Potato
Pancakes (page 132) and Maple Asian
Pear Applesauce (page 164), for a festive
dinner.

Serves 4 to 6

3 tablespoons goose fat (see headnote)
1 onion, finely chopped
1 carrot, peeled and finely chopped
3 garlic cloves, minced
1 large red cabbage (about 3½ to
   4 pounds), cored and shredded
2 green apples, such as pippin
   or Granny Smith, peeled, cored,
   and coarsely chopped
1 cup dry red wine

1½ cups chicken broth
1 bay leaf
A good pinch of ground nutmeg
A good pinch of ground cloves
1 tablespoon brown sugar
Salt and freshly ground black pepper
2 tablespoons red wine vinegar
1 tablespoon finely chopped fresh parsley
   for garnish

1 In a medium Dutch oven or flameproof casserole, heat the fat over medium heat. Add the onion and carrot and sauté for 5 to 7 minutes, or until softened. Add the garlic and sauté for another minute. Add the shredded cabbage and apples and cover the pot for 2 minutes to steam the cabbage and encourage it to soften. Remove the lid, toss the cabbage, and cook for 5 to 6 minutes, stirring occasionally, or until the cabbage is beginning to soften.

2 Add the wine, 1 cup of the broth, the bay leaf, spices, and sugar, and season with salt and pepper, stir to mix well, and cover the pot. Reduce the heat to very low and simmer gently for about 1 hour, or until the cabbage is very tender.

3 Add the remaining ½ cup broth and the vinegar and cook, covered, for 15 more minutes, or until the cabbage is nicely flavored and is soft. Remove the bay leaf, and taste for seasoning.

4 With a slotted spoon, transfer to a serving bowl. Garnish with the parsley, and serve.

ADVANCE PREPARATION
This may be made up to 2 days ahead, covered, and refrigerated. Reheat gently.

Roasted Jerusalem Artichokes and Carrots

During the fall and winter months, a platter of roasted vegetables is one of my signature dishes. Eaten raw, Jerusalem artichokes taste a bit like sweet crisp jicama; roasted unpeeled, they taste like a sweet root vegetable somewhere between a parsnip, turnip, and potato. Be sure to use a large shallow roasting pan to give the vegetables plenty of room for even cooking.

Serves 4 to 6

1 pound Jerusalem artichokes, cut into 2-inch chunks
1 pound carrots, peeled and cut into 2-inch chunks
6 scallions, white and light green parts only, sliced into 2-inch pieces
8 garlic cloves, peeled and root ends trimmed
2 tablespoons olive oil
1 teaspoon finely chopped fresh thyme
Salt and freshly ground black pepper
2 tablespoons finely chopped fresh parsley for garnish

1 Preheat the oven to 425°F. In a large shallow roasting pan, combine the vegetables, scallions, and garlic and toss to combine. Drizzle with the oil, add the thyme and season with salt and pepper, and toss well to coat all the vegetables evenly.

2 Roast for 40 minutes, turning the vegetables once. Continue roasting for 10 more minutes or until crisp, brown, and cooked through. Taste for seasoning.

3 Spoon the vegetables into a serving bowl and garnish with the parsley. Serve immediately.

ADVANCE PREPARATION
This may be prepared up to 4 hours ahead and kept, covered, at room temperature. Reheat in a 350°F oven for about 20 minutes.

Green Beans with Glazed Shallots and Lemon

→ *Glazed shallots and lemon* turn an everyday side dish into a festive addition to the dinner table. I like to serve this on holidays because both children and adults like it.

Serves 6 to 8

2 pounds small tender green beans, trimmed
2 tablespoons olive oil
6 shallots, thinly sliced

1 teaspoon finely chopped lemon zest
1 tablespoon fresh lemon juice
1 tablespoon finely chopped fresh parsley
Salt and freshly ground black pepper

1 Bring a large saucepan of salted water to a boil, add the beans, and cook for about 5 to 7 minutes, until tender but still slightly resistant. Drain in a colander, rinse the beans under cold water to stop the cooking, and drain well.

2 In a medium skillet, heat the olive oil over medium heat. When the oil begins to sizzle, add the shallots and sauté, stirring, for about 5 minutes, until glazed and golden brown. Add the beans and stir, then turn up the heat and continue stirring the beans for about 2 more minutes, until they just begin to brown. (Tongs work well for this.) Stir in the lemon zest and juice and cook for another 30 seconds. Add the parsley, season with salt and pepper, and toss to combine.

3 Place the beans in a serving dish and serve immediately.

ADVANCE PREPARATION
This may be made through Step 1 up to 8 hours ahead, covered, and refrigerated.

Braised Spinach with Leeks and Roasted Garlic

→ The leeks add sweetness to the bright green spinach, while the roasted garlic adds a nutty flavor.

Serves 4 to 6

2 tablespoons olive oil

2 medium leeks, white and light green parts only, cleaned and finely chopped

2 tablespoons Roasted Garlic Puree (page 163)

Salt and freshly ground black pepper

Two 12-ounce packages fresh baby spinach (or 1½ pounds baby spinach)

1 teaspoon fresh lemon juice

1 In a large Dutch oven, heat the oil over medium heat. Add the leeks and sauté for 3 to 5 minutes, or until soft. Add the garlic puree, season with salt and pepper, and sauté for another minute. Add half of the spinach, pushing it down to make it fit into the pan, and turn it with tongs to coat with the leek-garlic mixture. Cover tightly and steam for 2 to 3 minutes, turning the spinach with tongs after the first minute. Add the remaining spinach and turn with tongs to coat. Cover and cook for another 2 minutes, or until the second batch of spinach just begins to wilt.

2 Uncover the pot and cook, turning with tongs, for about 1 minute, until the spinach is wilted. There will be excess liquid from the spinach in the bottom of the pot, so drain the spinach carefully. Add the lemon juice and taste for seasonings.

3 Transfer to a serving bowl and serve immediately.

Potato and Onion Gratin

→ *A potato gratin* is a traditional French side dish. This variation features sliced potatoes layered with onion marmalade and finished with a garlicky cheese topping. Serve with Short Ribs with Dried Mushrooms and Fire-Roasted Tomatoes (page 74) or Braised Chicken with Caramelized Onions and Wild Mushrooms (page 56). With Green Beans with Glazed Shallots and Lemon (page 128), this makes a great vegetarian main course.

Serves 6 to 8

2 tablespoons olive oil
2 large onions, thinly sliced
1/2 teaspoon sugar
1 teaspoon balsamic vinegar
Salt and freshly ground black pepper
4 medium garlic cloves, minced
3 tablespoons finely chopped fresh parsley

2 cups grated Gruyère cheese
4 pounds russet (baking) or Yukon Gold potatoes, scrubbed and sliced into 1/4-inch-thick slices
2 cups chicken broth
2 tablespoons unsalted butter, cut into small pieces

1 In a large skillet, heat the olive oil over medium heat. Add the onions and sugar and sauté for about 15 to 20 minutes, or until the onions are browned and caramelized. Add the balsamic vinegar and cook for another 2 minutes, or until the vinegar is evaporated and the onions are very brown. Season with salt and pepper and set aside.

2 Preheat the oven to 375°F. Grease a 9-by-13-inch baking dish. In a small bowl, combine the garlic, parsley, cheese, and pepper to taste.

3 Layer half the potatoes in the bottom of the baking dish. Spread the onion mixture evenly over the potatoes. Season with salt and pepper. Sprinkle half of the cheese mixture evenly on top. Layer the remaining potatoes over the cheese and season with salt and pepper. Pour the chicken broth over the potatoes. Sprinkle the remaining cheese mixture evenly over the top and dot with the butter.

4 Cover the dish with buttered foil and bake for 30 minutes. Remove the foil and bake uncovered for 30 more minutes, or until the top is brown and crusty and the potatoes are fork-tender. Serve immediately.

ADVANCE PREPARATION
This may be made up to 4 hours ahead, covered, and left at room temperature. Reheat in a 375°F oven for 20 minutes, or until bubbling.

Rustic Mashed Potatoes
with Mascarpone and Chives

1 teaspoon salt, or to taste
3 pounds Yukon Gold potatoes, cut
   into 3-inch pieces
10 garlic cloves, peeled and root ends
   trimmed

⅓ cup mascarpone cheese
1 cup milk
3 tablespoons finely chopped fresh chives
White pepper

→ **Can there ever be** too many potato recipes? I don't think so. When I was writing my book *Potatoes,* I remember wondering how I would ever come up with enough recipes to fill a book. In fact, I could have gone on and on. This creamy-style mashed potato recipe uses both milk and mascarpone cheese for a slightly unusual flavor. Don't bother peeling the potatoes. I prefer Yukon Gold or Yellow Finn varieties for their creamy texture, but if you can't find them, try red or white boiling potatoes. Russets have a drier, fluffier texture.

Serves 6

1 Bring a large pot of water to a boil. Add the salt, potatoes, and garlic, reduce the heat, and simmer, covered, for about 15 to 20 minutes, until the potatoes are fork-tender.

2 Drain the potatoes and garlic in a colander and return to the pot. Dry the potatoes over high heat for 1 to 2 minutes, tossing them until all the moisture is evaporated. Transfer the potatoes and garlic to a large bowl and immediately mash the potatoes with a potato masher or an electric mixer. Add the mascarpone and milk and beat with a wooden spoon or wire whisk until smooth. When the liquid has been absorbed, add 2 tablespoons of the chives and salt and pepper to taste.

3 Transfer to a serving bowl, garnish with the remaining tablespoon of chives, and serve immediately.

ADVANCE PREPARATION
This may be prepared up to 2 hours ahead, covered, and kept at room temperature. Reheat gently in the top of a double boiler over medium heat, adding additional milk as needed. Taste for seasoning before serving.

Crispy Scallion-Potato Pancakes

→ *These pancakes are always* in high demand at my house. Whoever claims to be dieting falls off the wagon after a single taste of these crispy gems, topped with sour cream and fresh applesauce. Scallions add a hint of onion to the basic potato flavor. To make the pancakes crispy, not greasy, be sure the oil is very hot. The recipe doubles or triples easily if you're having a crowd.

Serve quarter-sized pancakes as an appetizer with a dab of crème fraîche, smoked salmon, and caviar. Or top the baby pancakes with a glistening of Chipotle Cream (page 161) and tiny shrimp. I also serve these for breakfast or brunch with scrambled eggs or a frittata.

Serves 4 to 6 (makes 12 to 14 pancakes)

6 scallions, white and light green parts only, thinly sliced
2 large eggs
2 medium russet (baking) potatoes, peeled and cut into 1-inch cubes
2 tablespoons matzo meal
Salt and freshly ground black pepper
Vegetable oil for frying
1 cup Maple Asian Pear Applesauce (page 164) **for serving**
1 cup sour cream for serving

1 In a food processor, process the scallions and eggs until smooth and fluffy. Add the potatoes and pulse until the potatoes are finely chopped but the mixture still retains some texture. Add the matzo meal, season with salt and pepper, and process briefly to combine; do not overprocess. Pour the batter into a medium bowl and let sit for 15 minutes, covered with plastic wrap to prevent discoloration.

2 In a large nonstick skillet, heat ¾ inch of oil over medium-high heat. Pour a scant tablespoon of batter into the skillet to test the oil (use a ladle, small ice cream scoop, or large tablespoon). If it is hot enough, the pancake will begin to sizzle and brown. Turn the pancake to brown the other side, then taste the pancake and check the seasoning; season the batter again if necessary.

3 Spoon tablespoons of the batter into the skillet, making sure there's a little room between each pancake, and flatten them with the back of the spoon. Use a spatula to round out the sides if necessary. Fry the pancakes for 2 to 3 minutes, or until they are golden brown on the first side, then turn them and brown the other side, about 2 more minutes. Transfer the pancakes to a cookie sheet lined with 2 layers of paper towels to drain. Repeat with the remaining batter.

4 Place the pancakes on a platter and serve with the applesauce and sour cream.

ADVANCE PREPARATION
The pancakes can be frozen for up to 1 month. To freeze, lay the cooled pancakes in a single layer on a sheet of aluminum foil, place another sheet of foil on top, and enclose them tightly in the foil. Place on a flat surface in the freezer. To serve, preheat the oven to 425°F. Place the foil packet of still-frozen pancakes on a baking sheet, and remove the top sheet of foil so that the pancakes will heat evenly. Bake for 5 to 7 minutes, until the pancakes are hot.

Yam Towers with Chipotle Chive Cream

➔ For a change from potatoes, try these slices of sweet yams. They add color and a spicy kick to your dinner menu. Serve with any simply grilled fish, chicken, or meat, or serve them next Thanksgiving for a new taste.

Serves 6 to 8

2 large yams (about 1½ pounds)—
choose evenly sized and shaped yams

2 teaspoons oil

2 tablespoons Chipotle Cream (page 161)
for serving

2 teaspoons very finely sliced fresh chives
for serving

1 Preheat the oven to 400°F. Wash the yams and rub lightly with the oil. Place on a baking sheet and bake for 30 minutes.

2 Prick the skin of each yam and return to the oven for 30 more minutes, or until tender.

3 Remove and discard the narrow pointed ends of the yams. Slice the yams into 2-inch-thick pieces.

4 Lay the pieces flat on a plate and garnish each with Chipotle Cream and chives. Serve immediately.

Roasted Fennel

When fennel is roasted, it takes on a subtle sweet taste. The leek and garlic cloves add a sweet caramelized flavor. Serve this as a side to any grilled or roasted entrée. No matter how much I make, there never seems to be enough.

Serves 4 to 6

4 fennel bulbs, trimmed, cored, and thinly sliced, feathery fronds reserved for garnish

1 leek, white and light green parts only, cleaned and finely chopped

10 garlic cloves, halved

3 tablespoons olive oil

Salt and freshly ground black pepper

Grated zest of 1 lemon

1 teaspoon fresh lemon juice

1 Preheat the oven to 425°F. In a shallow roasting pan, combine the fennel, leek, and garlic. Add the oil, season with salt and pepper, and toss with tongs to coat the vegetables evenly.

2 Roast, turning the fennel pieces and garlic a few times, for about 40 minutes, or until the fennel is softened, nicely browned, and caramelized.

3 Add the lemon zest and juice, toss to coat, and taste for seasoning. Place in a serving dish and garnish with the reserved fennel fronds.

ADVANCE PREPARATION

This may be made up to 4 hours ahead and kept, covered, at room temperature. Reheat in a 350°F oven for 10 to 15 minutes.

Corn Bread, Chestnut, and Dried Fruit Dressing

→ *Stuff your Thanksgiving turkey* with this savory fruit dressing, or serve it alongside in a casserole dish. Either way, the different tastes and textures make for a memorable addition to your Thanksgiving table. Make sure to dry the corn bread at least overnight before putting this together.

Serves 8 to 12
(makes enough to stuff
a 16-pound turkey)

6 cups cubed corn bread
3 tablespoons olive oil
3 tablespoons unsalted butter
1 onion, finely chopped
½ pound mushrooms, sliced
3 stalks celery, coarsely chopped
Salt and freshly ground black pepper
1 cup bottled steamed or roasted
  chestnuts, coarsely chopped

½ cup dried apricots, coarsely chopped
½ cup dried pitted prunes, coarsely
  chopped
½ cup finely chopped fresh parsley
2 teaspoons finely chopped fresh thyme
½ cup chicken or turkey broth, or
  as needed

1 The day before: Spread the corn bread on a baking sheet and let it sit out overnight to dry. Turn it at least once to dry it evenly.

2 Preheat the oven to 350°F. In a large skillet, heat the oil and butter over medium heat. Add the onion and sauté for about 5 minutes, or until nicely softened. Add the mushrooms and celery and sauté for about 4 more minutes, until the mushrooms are softened. Season with salt and pepper, and transfer the vegetables to a large bowl.

3 Add the chestnuts, apricots, prunes, parsley, thyme, and corn bread and mix to combine. Season with salt and pepper. Slowly add the broth, mixing carefully. The stuffing should be moist but not too compact if you are planning to use it to stuff a turkey. Taste for seasoning.

4 Grease a medium baking dish, and transfer the stuffing to it. Cover tightly with foil. Bake for 45 minutes.

5 Remove the foil and bake the stuffing for another 15 minutes, or until the top is brown. Serve immediately.

ADVANCE PREPARATION
This may be prepared through Step 4 up to 1 day in advance, covered, and refrigerated. Remove from the refrigerator 1 hour before baking.

DESSERTS

Apple, Pear, and Dried Cherry Almond Crisp

Toasted Coconut Cake

Chocolate Fudge Pie

Maple Walnut Tart

Mocha Truffle Tart

Chocolate Peanut Butter Brownies

Pumpkin-Chocolate Bread Pudding

Butterscotch Pudding

Citrus Pudding Cake

Persimmon Crostini with Honeyed Mascarpone and Pomegranate Seeds

Apple, Pear, and Dried Cherry Almond Crisp

→ **This dessert is a must** for your Christmas buffet. Apples, pears, and tart dried cherries form the basis of this cold-weather crisp, and the crème fraîche layer spread over the fruit becomes almost like custard. The almond topping crisps up beautifully, adding another distinct texture. Serve this just out of the oven or at room temperature.

Serves 6 to 8

½ cup dried cherries
3 medium Anjou pears, peeled, cored, and cut into 1½-inch pieces
3 medium Gala apples, peeled, cored, and cut into 1½-inch pieces
½ cup all-purpose flour
¼ cup sugar
1 cup crème fraîche

TOPPING
¾ cup all-purpose flour
⅓ cup packed brown sugar
¼ cup finely ground almonds
½ teaspoon salt
1 teaspoon pumpkin pie spice
1 teaspoon finely chopped lemon zest
1 teaspoon vanilla extract
½ cup (1 stick) unsalted butter, melted

1 Preheat the oven to 375°F. Grease an 8-by-10-inch or 9-by-12-inch gratin or baking dish.

2 Place the cherries in a bowl and pour over boiling water to cover. Let sit for 10 minutes to plump them, then drain.

3 In a bowl, mix together the cherries, pears, and apples. Add the flour and sugar and toss until the fruit is well coated. Transfer to the gratin dish. Spread the crème fraîche evenly over the fruit.

4 *To make the topping:* In a medium bowl, combine the flour, brown sugar, almonds, salt, pumpkin pie spice, and lemon zest and mix together. Add the vanilla and melted butter and mix until the consistency resembles a soft dough. With your fingers, crumble the mixture evenly over the fruit.

5 Bake for 55 minutes, or until the topping is golden brown and cooked through. Let rest for 10 minutes and then serve, or let cool to room temperature before serving.

ADVANCE PREPARATION
This may be prepared up to 8 hours ahead, covered, and kept at room temperature. Reheat in a 375°F oven for about 10 minutes before serving.

Toasted Coconut Cake

This is a wonderful cake for special occasions, the one a friend requests for his birthday every year. The cake is moist and not too sweet. The frosting is lighter than a traditional cream cheese style and more interesting than the classic Italian meringue. If you like soft coconut, just omit the toasting step.

Serves 10 to 14

One 7-ounce package sweetened
   decorating coconut

CAKE

3 cups cake flour
1 tablespoon baking powder
1/2 teaspoon salt
1 cup (2 sticks) unsalted butter, softened
2 cups sugar
4 large eggs
1/4 cup cream of coconut
1 cup sour cream

FROSTING

1 cup heavy (whipping) cream
1/2 cup sugar
Two 8-ounce containers (2 cups)
   mascarpone cheese, softened
1/2 cup cream of coconut

1/2 cup cream of coconut

1 Preheat the oven to 350°F. Grease and flour two 9-inch cake pans.

2 Toast the coconut: Spread the coconut evenly on a large baking sheet. Toast for about 10 to 12 minutes, tossing the coconut occasionally to brown it evenly, until golden brown. Let cool.

3 *To make the cake:* Sift together the flour, baking powder, and salt into a bowl.

4 In the bowl of an electric mixer fitted with the paddle attachment, or in a large bowl using a hand-held mixer, beat the butter and sugar for about 2 minutes, until light and fluffy. Add the eggs one at a time, beating until completely blended after each addition and scraping down the sides of the bowl. Add half of the flour mixture and then half of the cream of coconut and sour cream, beating until blended. Add the remaining flour, cream of coconut, and sour cream and beat until smooth.

5 Divide the batter between the cake pans and smooth the tops with a spatula. Bake for 30 to 35 minutes, or until a skewer inserted in the center comes out clean and the cake just begins to pull away from the sides of the pans. Let cool, then invert onto a cake rack and turn right-side up.

6 *To make the frosting:* In the bowl of an electric mixer fitted with the whip attachment, or in a large bowl using a hand-held mixer, whip the cream with the sugar until firm peaks form. In another large bowl whip the mascarpone with the cream of coconut until well blended. Add the whipped cream to the cheese mixture and blend together until well combined and light and fluffy.

CONTINUED

7 *To frost the cake:* Place one layer on a cake plate, with 3 or 4 strips of wax paper underneath the cake to keep the plate clean. Brush with ¼ cup of the cream of coconut, and spread a layer of frosting over the top. Sprinkle a little toasted coconut evenly over the layer. Place the second layer on top. Brush with the remaining ¼ cup cream of coconut. Frost the sides and then the top. With your hands, press some of the remaining toasted coconut onto the sides of the cake, then sprinkle the rest evenly on the top of the cake. Remove the wax paper and refrigerate until 30 minutes before serving.

ADVANCE PREPARATION
This may be made up to 8 hours ahead. (Remove from the refrigerator 30 minutes before serving.)

Chocolate Fudge Pie

→ *Some people* can never get enough chocolate desserts. This one is a cross between a pie and a fudgey brownie. If you are in a hurry, pick up a packaged crust in the refrigerated section of your market.

Serves 6 to 8

PASTRY
1 ¼ cups all-purpose or pastry flour
3 tablespoons confectioners' sugar
½ cup (1 stick) chilled unsalted butter, cut into small pieces
1 large egg yolk
About ¼ cup ice water

FILLING
¾ cup (1 ½ sticks) unsalted butter
3 ounces unsweetened chocolate
3 large eggs, lightly beaten
1 ½ cups granulated sugar
6 tablespoons all-purpose flour
½ teaspoon salt
1 tablespoon vanilla extract

1 *To make the pastry:* Combine the flour and confectioners' sugar in a food processor and pulse to blend. Add the butter and process for about 5 to 10 seconds, until the mixture resembles coarse meal. With the blades turning, gradually add the egg yolk and then enough water so the dough just begins to come together and will adhere when pinched. Shape the pastry into a disk, wrap in plastic, and chill for 20 minutes.

2 Preheat the oven to 375°F. Transfer the pastry to a floured pastry board or work surface. Roll the pastry out into a 12-inch circle. Drape the pastry circle over the rolling pin and fit it into the 9-inch pie pan, pressing against the bottom and sides to remove any air pockets. With a knife trim the excess dough to a ¾-inch overhang. Raise the edges of the pastry ¼ to ½ inch above the top of the pan by squeezing the dough with your thumb and index finger to flute the edges. Place the pie pan on a baking sheet. To prevent the pastry from rising, line it with a sheet of parchment paper or foil, pressing it against the sides, and fill with baking beads, dried beans, or rice.

3 Bake the crust for 15 to 18 minutes, or until crisp and lightly browned. Remove the paper or foil and weights and prick the bottom of the pastry shell with a fork. (The beans or rice may be reused.) Transfer the pie pan to a rack. Reduce the oven temperature to 350°F.

4 Meanwhile, make the filling: In a small heavy saucepan, combine the butter and chocolate and warm over low heat, stirring occasionally, until melted. Remove from the heat and let cool.

5 In a medium bowl, whisk together the eggs, sugar, flour, salt, and vanilla until smooth. Stir in the melted chocolate mixture and blend well.

6 Pour the filling into the baked shell. Bake for 40 to 45 minutes, or until the center is just set; a skewer inserted in the center should come out barely clean. Transfer to a rack to cool to room temperature.

ADVANCE PREPARATION
This is best the day it is baked, but it may be made up to 1 day ahead, covered, and kept at room temperature.

Maple Walnut Tart

➡ *Walnuts pair with maple syrup* in a sophisticated tart that tastes a bit like a Southern nut pie. The maple syrup infuses the dark corn syrup with its own identifiable sweetness. A dollop of maple whipped cream adds a complementary flavor and finish to the dessert.

Serves 6 to 8

PASTRY
1½ cups all-purpose flour
1 tablespoon confectioners' sugar
9 tablespoons chilled unsalted butter,
  cut into small pieces
About ¼ cup cold water

FILLING
3 cups walnuts
½ cup packed dark brown sugar
2 tablespoons all-purpose flour

Pinch of salt
½ cup good-quality maple syrup
½ cup dark corn syrup
3 large eggs
1 tablespoon unsalted butter, melted

Confectioners' sugar for garnish

MAPLE WHIPPED CREAM
1 cup heavy (whipping) cream
¼ cup maple syrup, chilled

1 *To make the pastry:* Combine the flour and confectioners' sugar in a food processor. Add the butter and process for 10 to 15 seconds, or until the mixture resembles coarse meal. With the blades turning, gradually add enough water so the dough just begins to come together and will adhere when pinched. Turn the dough out, knead it briefly together, and shape into a disk. Wrap in plastic and chill for 20 minutes.

2 *To make the filling:* Preheat the oven to 400°F. Place the walnuts on a baking sheet and toast them for about 7 to 10 minutes, or until lightly toasted. Set aside.

3 In a medium bowl, combine the brown sugar, flour, salt, maple syrup, corn syrup, eggs, and butter and whisk until thoroughly blended. Set aside.

4 Transfer the dough to a floured surface and roll it out into a circle large enough to line an 11-inch tart pan with a removable bottom. Drape the pastry over the rolling pin and fit it into the pan. Roll the rolling pin over the top of the tart pan with moderate pressure to remove excess overhanging dough. Press the pastry against the sides of the pan. Place the tart pan on a baking sheet.

5 Spread the walnuts in the tart shell. Pour in the filling. Bake for 15 minutes. Reduce the oven temperature to 350°F and bake for another 15 to 20 minutes, or until the pastry is browned and the filling is set. Transfer to a rack to cool.

6 Remove the sides of the pan and place the tart on a serving platter. Sprinkle with confectioners' sugar.

7 *To make the whipped cream:* In a medium bowl, combine the cream and maple syrup and whip with an electric mixer or a whisk until soft peaks form. Transfer to a serving bowl and serve on the side.

ADVANCE PREPARATION
The tart may be prepared up to 8 hours ahead, loosely covered, and left at room temperature. The cream may be prepared up to 2 hours ahead, covered, and refrigerated.

Mocha Truffle Tart

➥ *This is very rich* and very delicious. A little goes a long way, so slice into small servings. A smooth chocolate filling with just a touch of espresso is poured into a flaky baked crust. Swirled melted white chocolate adds a pretty design. Perfect for a holiday buffet or an elegant dinner, the tart can be served warm or at room temperature.

Serves 8 to 10

PASTRY
1 ¼ cups all-purpose or pastry flour
3 tablespoons confectioners' sugar
½ cup (1 stick) chilled unsalted butter, cut into small pieces
1 large egg yolk
About ¼ cup ice water

FILLING
¾ cup heavy (whipping) cream
¼ cup whole milk
1 tablespoon instant espresso powder

½ pound semisweet or bittersweet chocolate, such as Ghirardelli or bittersweet Valhrona, cut into small pieces
2 large eggs
3 tablespoons granulated sugar
Pinch of salt

WHITE CHOCOLATE SWIRL
2 ounces white chocolate, such as Baker's, Ghirardelli, or Lindt, finely chopped
2 tablespoons heavy (whipping) cream

½ cup crème fraîche for serving

1 *To make the pastry:* Combine the flour and confectioners' sugar in a food processor. Add the butter and process for 5 to 10 seconds, or until the mixture resembles coarse meal. With the blades turning, gradually add the egg yolk and then enough water so the dough just begins to come together and will adhere when pinched. Shape the pastry into a disk, wrap in plastic, and chill for 20 minutes.

2 Preheat the oven to 375°F. Transfer the pastry to a floured pastry board or work surface. Roll the pastry out into a circle large enough to fit into a 9-inch tart pan with a removable bottom. Drape the pastry circle over the rolling pin and fit it into the pan. Roll the rolling pin over the pan with moderate pressure to remove excess dough. Press the pastry against the sides of the pan. Place the tart pan on a baking sheet. To prevent the pastry from rising, line it with a sheet of parchment paper or foil, pressing it against the sides, and fill with baking beads, dried beans, or rice.

3 Bake the crust for 15 minutes. Remove the paper or foil and weights and prick the bottom of the pastry shell with a fork. (The beans or rice may be reused.) Return the crust to the oven and bake for 7 to 10 minutes longer, or until nicely browned. Let cool.

4 *To make the filling:* In a medium heavy saucepan, combine the cream, milk, and espresso powder and bring to a boil over medium-high heat. Remove from the heat. Add the chocolate and whisk until the chocolate is completely melted and smooth, about 5 minutes.

5 In a medium bowl, whisk together the eggs, sugar, and salt until well mixed. Whisk in the chocolate mixture and blend completely.

6 *To make the white chocolate swirl:* In a small heavy saucepan, combine the white chocolate with the cream and stir over low heat until completely melted. Or put in a small glass bowl and microwave for 1 minute, or until melted and smooth.

7 Pour the filling into the tart shell and smooth the top. Drizzle the white chocolate and, using a skewer or the tip of a sharp knife, swirl it into the dark chocolate in a feathery pattern.

8 Bake the tart for about 22 minutes, or until the filling is slightly puffed at the edges and a skewer inserted in the center comes out clean. Let stand on a rack for at least 15 minutes.

9 To serve: Using pot holders, remove the sides of the pan. Place the tart on a serving platter, and serve with the crème fraîche.

ADVANCE PREPARATION
The tart may be prepared up to 1 day ahead, covered with foil, and refrigerated. Remove from the refrigerator 1 hour before serving. It can also be reheated on a baking sheet in a 350°F oven for about 10 minutes.

Chocolate Peanut Butter Brownies

¾ cup all-purpose flour
½ teaspoon baking powder
½ teaspoon salt
¾ cup (1½ sticks) unsalted butter
4 ounces unsweetened chocolate,
  broken into pieces

¾ cup chunky peanut butter
2 cups granulated sugar
4 large eggs
1 teaspoon vanilla extract
Confectioners' sugar for garnish

→ *Whenever I whip these up,* I am amazed at how quickly they disappear. Chocolate and peanut butter have a natural affinity for each other. These are great with a glass of cold milk. Take these brownies to a picnic or to a back-to-school night.

Makes 24 brownies

1 Preheat the oven to 350°F. Butter a 9-by-13-inch baking pan.

2 Combine the flour, baking powder, and salt in a small bowl. Set aside.

3 In the top of a large double boiler, combine the butter and chocolate and melt over medium heat. Add ½ cup of the peanut butter and stir to blend. Remove from the heat.

4 Add the sugar to the chocolate mixture and whisk vigorously to blend; don't worry if the mixture looks grainy. Add the eggs and vanilla and whisk until completely incorporated. Add the flour mixture and whisk until just blended.

5 Place the remaining ¼ cup peanut butter in a microwave-safe glass dish and microwave for 15 seconds. Or place in the top of a double boiler over medium heat and heat until softened.

6 Pour the batter into the prepared pan. Dot the top of the batter with the softened peanut butter, and swirl it with a knife, making sure that it is evenly distributed. Bake for 25 to 30 minutes, or until a toothpick inserted into the center comes out slightly fudgey. Remove from the oven and let cool on a rack.

7 Just before serving, sprinkle lightly with confectioners' sugar. Slice into 2-inch square brownies.

ADVANCE PREPARATION
These may be prepared up to 1 day ahead and stored in an airtight container.

Pumpkin-Chocolate Bread Pudding

→ *Here Pumpkin-Chocolate Loaf* is elevated to an extravagantly rich bread pudding. Slices of the loaf are soaked in a spiced pumpkin custard with chocolate chunks throughout, so you get a double dose of chocolate and pumpkin. This may become a new holiday tradition at your house.

Serves 8 to 12

Pumpkin-Chocolate Loaf (page 22)

CUSTARD
4 large eggs
3 large egg yolks
1 cup granulated sugar
¾ cup canned pumpkin puree
3 cups half-and-half

2 teaspoons vanilla extract
1 teaspoon pumpkin pie spice

4 ounces bittersweet chocolate,
   cut into small chunks
Confectioners' sugar for garnish
Whipped cream or crème fraîche
   for serving (optional)

1 Preheat the oven to 375°F. Butter a 9-by-13-inch baking dish.

2 Slice the pumpkin loaf into ½-inch-thick slices. Arrange the slices, overlapping them, to fill the baking dish.

3 *To make the custard:* In a large bowl, with a hand-held electric mixer on medium speed, beat the eggs and egg yolks until frothy. Slowly add the sugar and beat the mixture until it is thick and lemon colored. Reduce the speed to low and add the pumpkin puree and half-and-half. Add the vanilla and pumpkin pie spice.

4 Ladle the custard over the pumpkin bread slices until the baking dish is filled to the top. Scatter the chocolate chunks all around the pudding, making sure that they are evenly distributed.

5 Set the baking dish in a larger baking pan and pour enough hot water into the pan to reach halfway up the sides of the dish. Place the pudding in the oven and bake for 40 to 45 minutes.

6 Using heavy oven mitts and a large spoon, push the bread down so the still-liquid custard rises in the dish. Spoon the custard evenly over the bread slices. Bake for about 10 more minutes, or until a skewer inserted into the center comes out barely clean. Let cool slightly on a rack.

7 Sprinkle the pudding with confectioners' sugar and spoon out onto dessert plates. Serve with whipped cream or crème fraîche, if desired.

ADVANCE PREPARATION
The custard may be made up to 1 day in advance. Refrigerate covered, and bring to room temperature before assembling. You may also prepare the dish through Step 4 up to 1 day in advance and refrigerate it before cooking. It will be a bit less custardy when baked, since the bread will have absorbed the custard.

Butterscotch Pudding

This grown-up version of the ultimate comfort dessert, based on one served at Portland's celebrated Wildwood restaurant, is just right for serving in front of a cozy fire. The touch of Scotch gives the pudding some punch. I like to serve this in old-fashioned parfait glasses.

Serves 8

CARAMEL SAUCE
¾ cup sugar
¼ cup water
¼ cup heavy (whipping) cream

½ cup packed light brown sugar
⅓ cup cornstarch
1 teaspoon salt

3 cups whole milk
4 large egg yolks
¼ cup (½ stick) unsalted butter, softened
2 tablespoons Scotch
2 teaspoons vanilla extract
½ cup chopped toffee bars (Skor are good)
Whipped cream for garnish

1 *To make the caramel sauce:* In a medium heavy saucepan (do not use a dark pan, or you will not be able to see the color of the caramel), combine the sugar and water and cook over low heat to dissolve the sugar. Turn up the heat and continually swirl the pan over the flame for about 5 to 8 minutes, until the mixture turns a dark golden brown. The mixture will be bubbly; if sugar crystals form on the sides of the pan, cover it for 1 minute to dissolve them. Watch carefully, as the caramel can burn easily. Remove the caramel from the heat and let it cool slightly; it should still be liquid.

2 Return the caramel to low heat and add the cream, whisking constantly until smooth. Let cool.

3 In a medium heavy saucepan, combine the brown sugar, cornstarch, and salt. Whisk in the milk, place over medium heat, and stir for about 5 to 6 minutes, or until the mixture becomes very thick. Remove from the heat and stir in the caramel sauce.

4 In a large bowl, whisk the egg yolks together; then slowly add the caramel mixture, whisking constantly, about 3 minutes. Pour back into the saucepan and gently heat the mixture until it easily coats the back of a spoon. Add the butter, Scotch, and vanilla and mix to combine.

5 Pour the pudding into individual glass dessert bowls. Sprinkle evenly with ¼ cup of the chopped toffee. Refrigerate for at least 8 hours.

6 Just before serving, garnish each pudding with a dollop of whipped cream and a sprinkling of the remaining chopped toffee.

ADVANCE PREPARATION
The pudding may be made up to 1 day ahead, covered tightly with plastic wrap, and refrigerated.

Citrus Pudding Cake

→ *This light, citrusy, homey dessert* is easy to make and quite welcome after a heavy meal. The mixture bakes up into a sponge cake on top with a pudding layer underneath. Depending on the baking dish you use, you will get different results. If you use a soufflé dish, there will be a larger proportion of pudding. If you use a rectangular baking dish, the dessert will look more like a light soufflé cake with a thin pudding layer on the bottom. I like to serve it warm, with a dollop of whipped cream.

Serves 4 to 6

$3/4$ cup, plus 2 tablespoons sugar
2 tablespoons unsalted butter, softened
2 teaspoons grated lemon zest
1 teaspoon grated lime zest
3 large eggs, separated
$1/4$ cup all-purpose flour

2 tablespoons strained fresh lemon juice
2 tablespoons strained fresh lime juice
1 cup half-and-half
$1/2$ cup heavy (whipping) cream,
    whipped to soft peaks (optional)
Fresh berries (optional)

1 Preheat the oven to 350°F. In a large bowl with a hand-held mixer, beat the $3/4$ cup sugar, the butter, and citrus zests together until creamy and well blended. Add the egg yolks and beat until blended. Alternately blend in the flour and the citrus juice, and half-and-half until well combined.

2 In a medium bowl, beat the egg whites with the remaining 2 tablespoons sugar until they form stiff, shiny peaks.

3 Fold the egg whites into the egg yolk mixture until just incorporated. Pour into a $1 1/2$-quart baking dish *(see headnote)*. Set the dish in a larger baking pan, and add enough hot water to the pan to reach halfway up the sides of the dish. Bake for 45 minutes, or until the top is set.

4 Serve hot, with whipped cream or berries, if desired.

Persimmon Crostini with Honeyed Mascarpone and Pomegranate Seeds

Twelve ½-inch-thick slices French bread
¼ cup mascarpone, softened
5 tablespoons fragrant honey, such as
  orange blossom, white truffle, or lavender

2 ripe Fuyu persimmons, peeled
  and thinly sliced
Seeds from ½ pomegranate

Fuyu persimmons are crisp, almost like an apple, and taste sweet. The orange persimmons and crimson pomegranate seeds garnish these dessert crostini with autumn colors. Look for an unusual honey to complement the crostini. These take just a few minutes to put together. Serve with a fruity dessert wine.

Serves 4 to 6

1 Preheat the oven to 350°F. Place the bread on a baking sheet and toast for about 7 minutes, or until lightly browned. Let cool.

2 In a small bowl, combine the mascarpone with 1 tablespoon of the honey and stir until blended and soft enough to spread.

3 Arrange the toasts on a platter and spread about a teaspoon of the mascarpone mixture on each toast. Arrange a few persimmon slices on top and sprinkle with a few pomegranate seeds. Lightly drizzle the remaining ¼ cup honey over the fruit. Serve immediately.

ADVANCE PREPARATION
The bread may be toasted up to 8 hours ahead and stored in an airtight container.

BASICS: *flavor enhancers, condiments, and sauces*

Perfect Pestos

→ **_Pesto is an important staple_** in my pantry. Although "pesto" (which translates as paste in Italian) usually refers to basil pesto, I am including three of my favorites here—pistachio, Mexican, and sun-dried tomato. These may be made up to 1 week ahead and refrigerated, but don't add the cheese until just before serving.

ADVANCE PREPARATION
Pesto recipes may be prepared up to 1 week ahead, tightly covered, and stored in the refrigerator.

Pistachio Pesto

Makes about 1¼ cups

½ cup raw pistachio nuts
3 medium garlic cloves, peeled
1½ cups firmly packed fresh Italian
   parsley leaves (about 1 medium bunch)
3 tablespoons finely chopped fresh chives
2 tablespoons fresh dill weed leaves
2 tablespoons fresh mint leaves

Grated zest of 1 lemon
½ cup olive oil
Freshly ground black pepper
¼ cup freshly grated Parmesan cheese
¼ cup freshly grated Pecorino Romano
   cheese

1 Preheat the oven to 350°F. Place the nuts on a small rimmed baking sheet and toast them for about 5 minutes, or until lightly browned and fragrant. Set aside.

2 With the motor running, add the garlic cloves to a food processor and process until minced. Add the herbs and lemon zest and process until finely chopped. Add the nuts and finely chop. With the blades turning, slowly pour in the olive oil in a fine stream. Scrape down the sides of the bowl and process again to blend the ingredients. Season with pepper. (If not using immediately, refrigerate the pesto in a tightly covered container until ready to use.)

3 Just before serving, add the cheeses and process until well blended. Taste for seasoning.

Mexican Pesto

Makes about 1¼ cups

½ cup raw pepitas (pumpkin seeds)
3 medium garlic cloves, peeled
1½ cups firmly packed fresh Italian
  parsley leaves (about 1 medium bunch)
1 cup fresh cilantro leaves

Grated zest of 1 lemon
½ cup olive oil
Freshly ground black pepper
½ cup freshly grated Parmesan cheese

1 Preheat the oven to 350°F. Place the seeds on a small rimmed baking sheet and toast them for about 5 minutes, or until lightly browned and fragrant. Set aside.

2 With the motor running, add the garlic cloves to a food processor and process until minced. Add the herbs and lemon zest and process until finely chopped. Add the seeds and finely chop. With the blades turning, slowly pour in the olive oil in a fine stream. Scrape down the sides of the bowl and process again to blend the ingredients. Season with pepper. (If not using immediately, refrigerate the pesto in a tightly covered container until ready to use.)

3 Just before serving, add the cheese and process until well blended. Taste for seasoning.

Sun-Dried Tomato Pesto

Makes about ½ cup

2 garlic cloves, peeled
½ cup oil-packed sun-dried tomatoes,
  drained (reserve the oil)
1 tablespoon oil reserved from the
  tomatoes, or more as needed

1 tablespoon balsamic vinegar
Salt and freshly ground black pepper

With the motor running, add the garlic to a food processor and process until minced. Add the tomatoes, the 1 tablespoon oil, and the vinegar, season with salt and pepper, and process until a thick paste is formed. If it is too thick, add a bit more oil. Taste for seasoning.

Chipotle-Garlic Puree

6 garlic cloves, peeled
One 7-ounce can chipotle chiles en adobo

➥ *I keep a jar of this* spicy smoky flavor enhancer in my refrigerator at all times to add to dressings, sauces, or any dish where I want an undertone of smoky heat.

With the motor running, add the garlic to a food processor and process until minced. Add the chiles, with their sauce, and process until totally pureed.

ADVANCE PREPARATION
This will keep for up to 1 month, covered tightly and stored in the refrigerator.

Makes about ¼ cup

Chipotle Cream

½ cup crème fraîche or sour cream
1 teaspoon **Chipotle-Garlic Puree** (facing page)
Salt and white pepper

→ *Use this as a dip,* or as a colorful layer of flavor swirled into soups, sauces, and salad dressings. Add a squirt of lime juice if you like.

In a small bowl, combine the crème fraîche and chipotle puree and mix well. Season with salt and pepper, and taste for seasoning.

Makes about ½ cup

ADVANCE PREPARATION
This may be prepared up to 3 days ahead, covered, and refrigerated.

Salsa Verde

→ **The tomatillo,** a relative of the Cape goose-berry, resembles a small green tomato. Tomatillos have a slightly lemony herb flavor. This alternative to spicy red salsa is milder and delicious in its own right. Try it with scrambled eggs, or on any grilled chicken or fish. If fresh tomatillos are unavailable, substitute a drained 12-ounce can of tomatillos.

Makes about 1¾ cups

NOTE
When working with chiles, always wear rubber gloves. Wash the cutting surface and knife right afterward.

1¾ cups chicken broth
¾ pound tomatillos, husked, rinsed, and diced
4 scallions, white and light green parts only, thinly sliced
2 medium garlic cloves, minced

2 jalapeño chiles, finely chopped (see Note)
¼ teaspoon ground cumin
2 teaspoons fresh lime juice
2 tablespoons chopped fresh cilantro
Salt

1 In a medium saucepan, combine the broth, tomatillos, scallions, garlic, half the chiles, and the cumin and bring to a boil over medium-high heat. Reduce the heat, partially cover, and simmer for about 15 minutes, or until slightly thickened. Let cool.

2 With a hand blender, coarsely puree the mixture, leaving some texture. Or transfer to a regular blender and coarsely puree. Add the remaining chiles, the lime juice, cilantro, and salt. Taste for seasoning.

ADVANCE PREPARATION
This may be made up to 5 days ahead, covered, and stored in the refrigerator. Remove from the refrigerator 30 minutes before serving.

Roasted Garlic Puree

60 garlic cloves, root ends trimmed
1 tablespoon olive oil

→ *This paste provides* a slightly nutty, creamy flavor boost for sauces, dressings, and vegetables. You can find large containers of peeled fresh garlic cloves in the refrigerated section of the produce department.

Makes about ¼ cup

1 Preheat the oven to 425°F. Place the garlic cloves on a large piece of heavy-duty foil. Sprinkle with the oil, and wrap tightly in the foil.

2 Place the package on a baking sheet and bake for 45 minutes to 1 hour, or until the garlic is soft when pierced with a knife. Remove from the oven and let cool.

3 Place the cloves in a small bowl and mash with a spoon, or process in a food processor until smooth.

ADVANCE PREPARATION
This may be prepared up to 1 week ahead, covered, and refrigerated.

Maple Asian Pear Applesauce

4 medium Asian pears, peeled, cored,
and cut into 1-inch chunks

4 medium pippin or Granny Smith apples,
peeled, cored, and cut into 2-inch chunks

¼ cup sugar

2 tablespoons maple syrup, or to taste

1 tablespoon fresh lemon juice, or to taste

→ *This unusual applesauce* has a pure apple flavor with a hint of maple syrup. The Asian pears must be cut smaller than the apples because they are firmer and take longer to cook. I like to serve this as a compote for brunch, with Crispy Scallion-Potato Pancakes (page 132), or for dinner with Short Ribs with Dried Mushrooms and Fire-Roasted Tomatoes (page 74) or Sauerbraten (page 73).

Makes about 4 cups

1 In a heavy nonaluminum saucepan, combine all the ingredients and set over medium heat. Cover and simmer for about 12 minutes, or until the apples are slightly softened.

2 Remove the lid and continue cooking, stirring occasionally to break up the larger pieces (you can use a potato masher if needed), for about 7 to 10 minutes, until the apples are soft but there is still some texture. Adjust the seasoning with maple syrup or lemon juice. Let cool, then cover and refrigerate.

ADVANCE PREPARATION

This may be prepared up to 1 week ahead, covered, and refrigerated.

Cranberry Fruit Chutney

→ *This chutney goes well* with many dishes besides the traditional turkey. Try it on grilled chicken or roast pork.

Makes about 4 cups

One 12-ounce bag fresh cranberries, picked over
1 Bosc pear, peeled, cored, and cut into 1-inch pieces
1 Fuji apple, peeled, cored, and cut into 1-inch pieces
1 onion, finely chopped
Grated zest of 2 lemons

1 teaspoon finely chopped fresh ginger
1 teaspoon dried mustard
½ teaspoon ground coriander
1 cup orange marmalade
½ cup packed brown sugar
3 tablespoons balsamic vinegar
¼ cup tawny port
Crushed red pepper flakes to taste

In a large nonaluminum saucepan, combine all of the ingredients, set over medium heat, and stir to mix well. Cover and cook for about 15 to 20 minutes, until the mixture begins to thicken and the fruit is softened. Remove from the heat and let cool, then taste for seasoning. Cover and refrigerate.

ADVANCE PREPARATION
This will keep for up to 1 month, tightly covered and stored in the refrigerator.

Balsamic Syrup

2 cups balsamic vinegar

→ *This is one of a cook's best friends.* You'll find it will perk up soups, sauces, and salads, even fruit and cheese.

Place the vinegar in a small heavy saucepan and bring to a boil over high heat. Boil the vinegar for about 12 to 14 minutes, or until it becomes syrupy; bubbles will begin to form. (Be careful not to reduce it too much, or it will burn.) Let cool.

Makes about ¾ cup

ADVANCE PREPARATION
This will keep for up to 1 month, covered, at room temperature.

Basic (or Balsamic) Vinaigrette

1 medium shallot, finely chopped

1 garlic clove, minced

1 teaspoon whole-grain mustard

3 tablespoons red wine vinegar

1 tablespoon fresh lemon juice

¾ cup olive oil

Salt and freshly ground black pepper

→ *This is my all-purpose salad dressing.* If you like the full-bodied flavor of balsamic vinegar, you can replace half of the red wine vinegar with balsamic. For a creamier version, you can also add a tablespoon or two of non-fat plain yogurt.

Makes 1 cup

In a medium bowl, combine the shallot, garlic, mustard, vinegar, and lemon juice and whisk until well blended. (Or place in a food processor and process until well blended.) Slowly add the olive oil, whisking continuously (or processing) until blended. Season with salt and pepper.

ADVANCE PREPARATION

This may be prepared up to 1 week ahead, covered, and refrigerated. Bring to room temperature and whisk well before using.

SUGGESTED MENUS

AUTUMN DINNER PARTY

Mushroom Soup with Port

Braised Chicken with Caramelized Onions and Wild Mushrooms

Roasted Fennel

Steamed baby potatoes

Mocha Truffle Tart

TAILGATE PICNIC

White Bean and Arugula Stew Gratinée

Grilled assorted sausages

Marinated Roasted Beets with Orange-Balsamic Vinaigrette

Belgian Endive Salad with Apples, Toasted Walnuts, and Fig Vinaigrette

Chocolate Peanut Butter Brownies

THANKSGIVING OR CHRISTMAS DINNER

Warm apple cider and Champagne

Butternut Squash and Chestnut Soup with Chipotle Cream

Roasted Hoisin Turkey Breast with Cranberry Fruit Chutney and Make-ahead Gravy

Corn Bread, Chestnut, and Dried Fruit Dressing

Rustic Mashed Potatoes with Mascarpone and Chives

Roasted Jerusalem Artichokes and Carrots

Green Beans with Glazed Shallots and Lemon

Pumpkin-Chocolate Bread Pudding or Persimmon Crostini with Honeyed Mascarpone

and Pomegranate Seeds

French Onion and Fennel Soup, page 44

AFTER THANKSGIVING PARTY

Turkey Potpie with Puff Pastry Crust

Marinated Roasted Beets with Orange-Balsamic Vinaigrette

Pumpkin-Chocolate Loaf

HANUKAH

Crispy Scallion-Potato Pancakes

Maple Asian Pear Applesauce

Rosemary-Orange Glazed Chicken

Green Beans with Glazed Shallots and Lemon

Chocolate Fudge Pie

NEW YEAR'S EVE

Mini Crispy Scallion-Potato Pancakes with smoked salmon and caviar

Champagne or sparkling wine

Winter Squash and Red Swiss Chard Risotto or Grapefruit, Mushroom,

and Avocado Salad

Grilled entrecôte with Chipotle Cream

Steamed broccoli florets

Mocha Truffle Tart

HOLIDAY BRUNCH

Sparkling wine with pomegranate juice and sliced oranges

Holiday Vegetable Strata

Grilled assorted sausages

Cinnamon-Streusel Sour Cream Coffee Cake

Fresh fruit salad with orange, apples, pears and Fuyu persimmons,

with maple yogurt

SUNDAY FOOTBALL LUNCH

Roasted vegetable platter

Spicy Chicken Gumbo with steamed rice

Toasted Coconut Cake

HEARTY SNOW COUNTRY BREAKFAST

Mixed orange, grapefruit, and cranberry juice

Breakfast Polenta with Mascarpone and Maple Syrup

Crisp bacon

VALENTINE'S DINNER

Fire-Roasted Tomato and Eggplant Bisque

Veal Chops with Grand Café Tapenade

Braised Spinach with Leeks and Roasted Garlic

Citrus Pudding Cake

RAINY DAY LUNCH

Hearty Lentil Soup with Grilled Sweet and Hot Italian Sausages

Open-Faced Grilled Cheese and Tomato Sandwiches

Pumpkin-Chocolate Loaf with sliced Fuji apples

WINTER DINNER PARTY

Mushroom Soup with Port

Sauerbraten

Braised Red Cabbage with Red Wine

Rustic Mashed Potatoes with Mascarpone and Chives

Apple, Pear, and Dried Cherry Almond Crisp

SOUP'S ON

Ribollita

Assorted French and rustic rolls with Grand Café Tapenade

Butterscotch Pudding

PASTA PRONTO

Sliced Fennel Salad with Lemon Parmesan Dressing

Fusilli with Pink Vodka Sauce and Velvet Chicken

Sliced pears with Gorgonzola dolcelatte

BY THE FIRESIDE COZY DINNER

French Onion and Fennel Soup

Belgian Endive Salad with Apples, Toasted Walnuts, and Fig Vinaigrette

Persimmon Crostini with Honeyed Mascarpone and Pomegranate Seeds

ELEGANT BIRTHDAY DINNER

Mixed greens with cherry tomatoes, toasted pepitas, and Balsamic Vinaigrette

Roast Chicken Breasts with Mexican Pesto Sauce

Butternut Squash and Corn Enchiladas with Salsa Verde and Chipotle Cream

Toasted Coconut Cake

WEEKNIGHT DINNER

Chicken Paillards with Pistachio Pesto Vinaigrette

Autumn Noodles and Rice

Roasted Jerusalem Artichokes and Carrots

Sliced pears with Explorateur cheese and drizzled honey

EASY DINNER PARTY

Frisée Salad with Bacon and Goat Cheese

Whole Roasted Striped Bass with Roasted Vegetables

Braised Spinach with Leeks and Roasted Garlic

Citrus Pudding Cake

LEISURELY WEEKEND LUNCH

Grapefruit, Mushroom, and Avocado Salad

Onion, Leek, and Olive Tart

Assorted sliced breads (seeded, currant or raisin, and French)

Sliced apples and pears, with wedges of blue and fresh goat cheese

MAKE-AHEAD DINNER

Winter greens with Basic Vinaigrette

Braised Lamb Shanks with Toasted Almond Gremolata

Couscous with Leeks, Currants, and Mint

Braised Spinach with Leeks and Roasted Garlic

Maple Walnut Tart

Index

Table of Equivalents

The exact equivalents in the following tables have been rounded for convenience.

Liquid/Dry Measures

U.S.	METRIC
¼ teaspoon	1.25 milliliters
½ teaspoon	2.5 milliliters
1 teaspoon	5 milliliters
1 tablespoon (3 teaspoons)	15 milliliters
1 fluid ounce (2 tablespoons)	30 milliliters
¼ cup	60 milliliters
⅓ cup	80 milliliters
½ cup	120 milliliters
1 cup	240 milliliters
1 pint (2 cups)	480 milliliters
1 quart (4 cups, 32 ounces)	960 milliliters
1 gallon (4 quarts)	3.84 liters
1 ounce (by weight)	28 grams
1 pound	454 grams
2.2 pounds	1 kilogram

Length

U.S.	METRIC
⅛ inch	3 millimeters
¼ inch	6 millimeters
½ inch	12 millimeters
1 inch	2.5 centimeters

Oven Temperature

FAHRENHEIT	CELSIUS	GAS
250	120	½
275	140	1
300	150	2
325	160	3
350	180	4
375	190	5
400	200	6
425	220	7
450	230	8
475	240	9
500	260	10